Soul Search

Soul Search

Thoughts Along The Way
From Religious Belief
To Spiritual Reality

With

Rosalie Allen Taylor

 www.trafford.com

North America & international
toll-free: 1 888 232 4444 (USA & Canada)
fax: 812 355 4082

In memory . . .

of Ralph, whose suggestion resulted
in the form of this book.

With caring . . .

For Erin Faith and her friends, who give
us hope for the future of our planet.

CONTENTS

Preface

*T*he road to discovering and trusting our spiritual/creative nature is usually crooked, rocky, and full of road–blocks of various sorts and sizes. In response to the rocks and blocks, our souls persist in calling attention to the importance of such discovery and trust through a variety of experiences – experiences which can reveal our dis–ease when we try to live in alienation from our own souls. Too seldom do we recognize that the symptoms of illness and depression are just that, and not the underlying problem. Too often we treat the symptoms without ever addressing the real issues of failing to give creative expression to the persons we are. In our work and in our relationships, we choose the safety of the conforming way over the vitality of the creative way, losing touch with our souls and denying our spirituality.

In the following pages I offer a "moving picture" of the process of following my own rocky road in an attempt to retrace my experiences and learnings as I have found my way to my present perspectives. Some of the writing is current thinking, some reflects on the past, and most but not all appears in its original form with little or no editing. I include personal thoughts and experiences related to blocks along the way, the persistence of the soul to the point of crisis, and the gradual formation of new ways of seeing our human situation.

Some experiences will be repeated in several papers, written at different times and for different purposes, as important to the continuity of those papers and thus not removed from the existing context. Hopefully those repetitions will not become offensive. Another possible problem is that the various papers do not follow in a nicely ordered procession, which follows from the fact that life itself is seldom an orderly procession. This is a collection of thoughts occurring at various times and under differing circumstances, with some thoughts probably more useful than others. This is most certainly not an exhaustive treatise or a final statement.

Presented within a current narrative are published articles, course assignments, correspondence, and some essays that have yet to see the light of day – a melange of writings usually drawn from particular time frames and changing perspectives and *occasionally organized around specific topics. They were written at many stages along the way as I moved beyond the barriers of traditional ways of thinking. It is surely my intention to continue to move beyond dogmatic thinking, and I invite you to do the same as we reconnect with our souls and reclaim our vital, spiritual, compassionate natures. Nothing less can save us from the alienation and violence of our present personal, social, and planetary predicaments.*

On a more personal note, I need to say that while I am a writer (anyone who writes is a writer!), I am not one who especially loves the process of writing. (I prefer drawing house plans.) I think of my friend Edna as a "real" writer, a woman who is now ninety–nine years old and has loved the process of writing since she was a teen–ager. Her published articles and books are well known in Canada, and she received the Order of Canada at age ninety. She did say once, perhaps jokingly, that she was prouder of getting her driver's license renewed at ninety than of the Order of Canada. Now, although she is no longer writing, she reads great numbers of books for an award she gives every year for creative non–fiction.

As for me, required writing assignments during my school and college years were always painful tasks, perhaps because I had nothing original to say. I did receive second prize in an essay contest my senior year in school, but I think it may have been because the judges were relieved to find a humorous piece in an otherwise sea of seriousness. It was only in my early thirties that I began to write in order to express my own ideas, and then with no intention to publish. Publication came later.

Recently I plucked a book off the shelf entitled THE COURAGE TO GROW OLD, *edited by Phillip L. Berman. It is a collection of writings by over forty older people, many of them writers and artists with words of encouragement. Some speak passionately of the importance of spirit, and one writer, Phyllis A. Whitney, speaks to my heart when she says it is never too late to write a book. She is aware of writing careers begun after age seventy! With this sense of spirit in mind, I venture forth at age eighty to put my thoughts "out there" in the following pages.*

PROLOGUE

Kairos: The Time is Now

The following statement was authored by George B. Leonard and Michael Murphy on behalf of the Esalen Insitute and was presented by George Leonard as the introduction to a talk by Abraham Maslow. The event took place at Grace Cathedral, San Francisco, on January 6, 1966, a moment in time during a decade described by Walter Truett Anderson as "young and full of hope". While the excesses of those years may have disappeared, the hope and the challenge remain.

On this night of the festival of Epiphany, we gather to celebrate a new *kairos*, a joyful and awesome moment in humankind's long day. Kairos. History unfolding like a bursting star. The present opening upon itself so that every scientist may become a seer, every academic a prophet. Kairos. A time when ten thousand voices in a multitude of strange new tongues struggle to utter a single thought: *the atom's soul is nothing but energy. Spirit blazes in the dullest clay. The life of every person – the heart of it – is pure and holy joy.*

How can we speak of joy on this dark and suffering planet? How can we speak of anything else? We have heard enough despair. We have heard enough of the same sick old doctrine of Original Sin. Those who dismay at humanity's condition have had their turn upon the stage. They have offered intricate critiques, sinuous analyses of everything that is wrong with humankind, leaving unanswered only the questions they have almost forgotten how to ask: What do we do now? How do we change it all? How do we act to make our society and ourselves whole? At a time when at last we have all the means at hand to end war, poverty and racial insanity, the prophets of despair discover no vision large enough to lead us to the merely possible.

This is a time for action, not analysis. No one of us can sleep secure while others suffer. Every one of us must go on working in the usual and political ways to help reduce the fever that saps us of our natural joy. But this is not enough. We must not just ameliorate our heritage of pain; we must create

1

anew. We must not merely analyze maladies; we must show people the way to-wards their own true selves so that, filled with the joy of learning, loving and being, they will study war and hatred no more. We must build new societies that seek not empires on the face of the earth, but ever–receding frontiers in the infinitely rich and varied countryside of humanity.

Listen to the new voices in a time of *kairos*. Here is what they are say-ing: Ever since humanity learned to think and hope, human beings have been haunted by an irrepressible dream – that the limits of human ability lie beyond the boundaries of the imagination; that each of us uses only a fraction of our abilities; that there must be some way for everyone to achieve far more of what is possible to achieve. History's greatest prophets;, mystics and saints have dreamed even more boldly, saying that all people are somehow one with God. The dream has survived history's failures, ironies and uneven triumphs, sustained more by intuition than by facts.

Now, however, the facts are beginning to come in. Science has at last turned its attention to the central questions of human capabilities. Look-ing deep into the brain, it finds unsuspected wave forms so subtle and complex as to suggest that, for all practical purposes, the human creative capacity is infinite. Looking afresh into human action, it finds new ways for ordinary people to achieve what appears to be miracles of feeling and doing. It is a beginning, a glimmering, a curtain opening: What the mys-tics promised is upon us now, not out on some apocalyptic plain, but in the laboratory, the church, the classroom, the home. Here is the century's biggest news: If we read it right, life on this planet will never again be the same.

Tonight we speak for scientists, religious leaders, educators and inter-ested citizens who have cast their lot with the future. We believe that all persons somehow possess a divine potentiality; that ways may be worked out – specific, systematic ways – to help, not the few, but the many towards a vastly expanded capacity to learn, to love, to feel deeply and to cre-ate. We reject the tired dualism that seeks God and human potentialities by denying the joys of the senses, the immediacy of unpostponed life. We believe that most people can best find God and themselves through heightened awareness of the world, increased commitment to the eternal in time.

We believe, too, that if the divine is present in the individual soul, it must be sought and found in our institutions as well; for people will not readily achieve individual salvation without a saving society. We envisage no mass movement, for we do not see people in the mass; we look instead to revolution through constant interplay between individual and group, each changing the other.

The revolution has begun. Human life will be transformed. How it will be transformed is up to us.

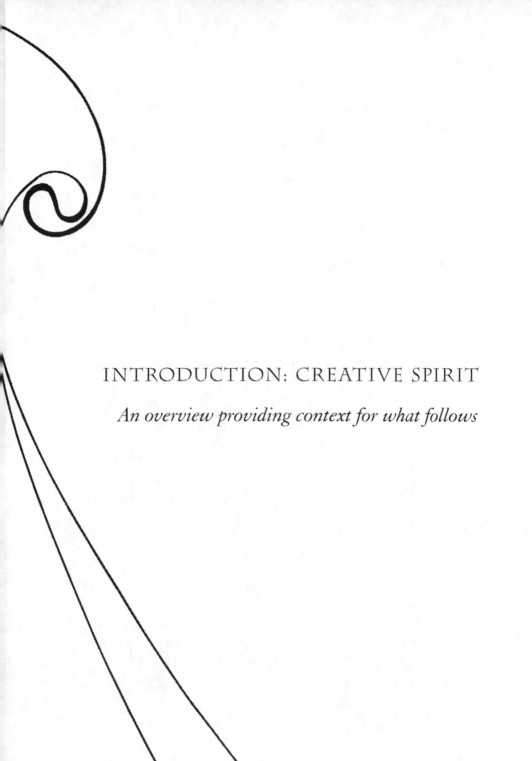

INTRODUCTION: CREATIVE SPIRIT

An overview providing context for what follows

At rare moments in our lives we may feel that we are in synchrony with the whole universe. These moments may occur under many circumstances – hitting a perfect shot at tennis or finding the perfect run down a ski slope, in the midst of a fulfilling sexual experience, in contemplation of a great work of art, or in deep meditation. These moments of perfect rhythm, when everything feels exactly right and things are done with great ease, are high spiritual experiences in which every form of separateness or fragmentation is transcended.

Fritjof Capra,
THE TURNING POINT

When things are falling apart, the advice usually given is retrace our steps, reclaim the former wisdom and return to the sure, predictable pathway. Apart from often being downright impractical, this may be intellectually, emotionally and spiritually destructive. At the crisis points of life, regression is rarely healthy. The crisis is an opportunity to make new strides forward, often into unknown territory.

Diarmuid O'Murchu,
RELIGION IN EXILE,
A Spiritual Homecoming

After hours of careful listening, my therapist offered an image that helped me eventually reclaim my life. "You seem to look upon depression as the hand of an enemy trying to crush you," he said "Do you think you could see it instead as the hand of a friend, pressing you down to ground on which it is safe to stand?"

Parker J. Palmer,
LET YOUR LIFE SPEAK,
Listening to the Voice of Vocation

ollowing is a brief paper which I wrote several years ago as a hand–out for a course on spirituality offered at a public library. My purpose in including it here is to provide a context for the writings that follow. Without it, the writings could seem too disconnected and unrelated to my own life process over a period of nearly fifty years.

INTRODUCTION

INTRODUCTION

Creative Spirit

MORE THAN TEN YEARS AGO I read a book by John Briggs entitled *FIRE IN THE CRUCIBLE*. I was very impressed with what the author had to say about the nature of creativity and genius, especially the former (as evidenced by much underlining on my part), but then consigned the book to the shelf with many other valuable volumes. There it remained until a few nights ago when I was searching for some bedtime reading and picked it out from among many others for a re–read. What I found in those pages stimulated my own thinking about creativity, a topic which has been of primary interest to me for over forty years.

A key chapter in a book–in–progress, with which I have been struggling for too long, relates my own experience of coming into a creative mode of living after passing most of my life until age thirty–one in what I call the "restrictive" mode. Cliff Havener, author of MEANING: THE SECRET OF BEING ALIVE, refers to these two modes respectively as the "integrative" and "normative", with the normative being the condition of the great majority of people in most (if not all) cultures of the world.

Another term I have used for the restrictive/normative mode is the "performance" mode. From the time we are very young, most of us have been forced to choose between self–expression and performing to please others. Vital to our survival are both the need to be who we are and the need to be loved and accepted by others. A few cling doggedly to being who they are, often experiencing the pain of ostracism from family and society and sometimes becoming angry enough to take out their anger in violent acts.

Those of us who choose to please others often lose touch with the soul self, not even knowing what we have lost. The result is often depression or worse, since in losing touch with our souls, we cut ourselves off from the natural creative energy of the universe or cosmos. Unless we wake up to our loss and choose to re–connect with our soul–self, we may go to our death without ever having lived the life we've been given.

Recently I have become aware that in writing what was first an article and which later became a key chapter in a book, I failed to place sufficient emphasis on the shifts in awareness which were the consequences of coming through the most crucial crisis of my life. I did indeed write about these shifts, but I failed to highlight them and expound on them in such a way as to relay the passionate nature of the experience and the dramatic consequences of new awareness. Reading John Briggs' words reinforced my consciousness of this failure.

Rather than repeat the whole chapter in which I relate the full story of my experience, perhaps a recap of the most important issues will be sufficient.

Prior to the crisis, I had been living a "normative, restrictive" suburban life as the wife of a lawyer, mother of two young children, and a community volunteer. Although a college graduate, I had been raised by my parents to be the wife of a successful man, not a career success in my own right, and my husband strongly seconded this view. Perhaps he thought he would appear "inadequate" if his wife worked outside the home, which was a fairly common attitude in the 50s, and I was so unsure of myself in any career sense that I welcomed the position allotted to me. So it was that I adopted the role that had been set out for me.

Warnings

During the fall of 1956, I began to sense that all was not well in the life I was leading. I felt "divorced" from my husband who was "married" to his successful career, somewhat estranged from my two children, weary of all my volunteer activities, and feeling that my life was going nowhere. Without any sense of purpose, my life seemed to be not only a waste of time and energy, but a terrible hoax. As Christmas approached, I felt none of the usual anticipation, and on the holiday itself, none of the inspiration of participating in choral church services as in the past.

While I never contemplated suicide, I simply did not care whether I lived or died. I did not consider asking for psychological help, perhaps because I had written off my studies in psychology after a professor had committed suicide following a final exam my senior year in college. Feeling torn by demands coming from many directions, I somehow knew that I just wanted to *be* without having to *do*.

Awareness

It was in this very depressed state, early in February 1957, that I recalled something a special Sunday school teacher had said to our little class of seventh graders twenty years earlier. She told us that God loved us the way we were, not the way we ought to be, or something to that effect. Having a rather logical turn of mind, I decided that it would be a good idea to put all my eggs in God's basket, whatever that might mean. I could let go of all the wearying demands, the satisfaction of which seemed to determine the worth of my person, and just let myself be. It was a terrifying choice, since I did not know whether I would then be loved or be worth anything at all.

Choice

Thus it was that one evening I went to the old chapel on our church grounds, knelt in the dark silence of the familiar surroundings, took what felt like a terrifying step into the unknown, and asked a seemingly remote God to take over my life. Strange as it seemed to me at the time, I immediately experienced a great sense of relief, uttered a brief prayer of thanks, and went home to bed.

I awoke the next morning to a whole new world of colors and sounds, tastes and scents with energy that I had not felt as long as I could remember

– and most especially, *delight in life.* In retrospect I would say that the flow of energy, which was formerly consumed by my unrecognized anxiety about having to *earn* my self–worth, was now free for living. Also, energy which was fragmented as I felt pulled in many directions was now concentrated in one direction. I experienced my worth in my *being* rather than in my *doing.* In time I would come to see that doing which proceeds from being is far more valuable to the human community and the planet because it involves our own unique talents, motivations, and vision of the whole rather than the tunnel vision of the alienated self. When we come from our being, we can "follow our bliss", to quote Joseph Campbell. Following our bliss means doing what engages the most we have to offer, our best talents and motivations, as our gift to life.

Consequences

In making such a shift from our doing/performance selves to living in the creative or integrative mode, we discover many changes in how we perceive and experience life. Some of these changes are immediate, or almost so, while others occur over months or even years. For me, the immediate changes were in the following areas:

- **Creativity.** I began to see all kinds of connections which I had never noticed previously, apparently because I had needed to accommodate my perceptions to the expectations of others for their approval. I could now give expression to my own ideas in many different ways, including writing, for at last I had something to say and thoughts worth sharing (well, many of them but not all of them!). I came to see the creative process as life itself, the way of the cosmos, the way of nature, of which we are meant to be both part and expression. It is what many call "open system living".

- **Meaning.** Overnight the terrible sense of meaninglessness disappeared, which was quite a surprising and even overwhelming experience. While I could not have told you what that meaning was, I knew without any question that I had begun living a meaningful life, which I now believe was a natural consequence of moving into the creative, open system mode. We find more specific meaning in different ways as we apply our particular talents in work and relationships.

- **Spirit.** My understanding of spirit changed dramatically, from a rather abstract principle to the experience of energy and consciousness which comes with living from the soul–self, the being self, the real self. For me, this is not a constant level but varies as I move from one situation to another. Some situations are life–enhancing, allowing and even encouraging us to be who we are and bringing out the best we have to offer, while others are deadening. Some writers, such as Linda Marks   (*LIVING WITH VISION: RECLAIM-ING THE POWER OF THE HEART*), equate spirituality and creative living, or at least say they are inseparable.

• **Connection.** Prior to the crisis experience, I had felt myself to be a separate and insignificant speck in the universe, a very lonely feeling. Afterwards I had a profound and lasting sense of being one with all that is, and also of being called to play my own unique part in the ongoing creative life of community and planet. This new sense of connection included an attitude of utmost respect for myself, others and nature as participants in the creative life. I no longer found my identity in any group or religion or political party, but in humanity as a whole. I experienced myself as an integral part of what some call the web of life.

• **Health.** I came to realize almost immediately that while living in the doing or performance mode, my body was always functioning under a certain amount of tension. While I was young enough not to have had any serious problems (only lingering colds and coughs in the winter and a degree of constipation ––"up tightness"!), now all my systems seemed to be flowing together in a natural way. While there have been times when parts of my body have tightened up again under stress, the general state has been one of relaxation. It also seems to me that living from being, or saying "yes" to life, has a beneficial effect on the immune system.

• **Religion.** Because I still considered myself a Christian, I began to read the Bible and other spiritual writings on my own, but with an eye to what rang true for me as guides to living. One example was the statement attributed to Jesus when he said that it was "expedient that I go away that the Holy Spirit come and dwell in you and teach you all things". For me, this meant that we were to trust the spirit within, not hang on to and idolize Jesus. I gave up on the kind of god which had been presented to me in the church, and when I studied the Old Testament at an Episcopal/Anglican seminary, it was the prophets who spoke to me. I read books on many different religions, but for the most part, their doctrines left me cold. Eventually I admitted to myself that church services no longer enhanced my life and even proved offensive to my sense of being. Worship became a matter of living my life to the fullest as my contribution to community, and communion was now a deep, real–life relationship with others.

- **Relationships.** With the shift in my sense of self worth from outer doing to inner being, many of my relationships changed rather dramatically. In the case of my children, I no longer based the relationship on getting them to love me (I already loved myself) and so could love them enough to set limits without concern for their reaction. They could no longer manipulate me, which was a great relief to me and eventually to them. As for my husband, I no longer nagged him to behave in certain ways so that what he did or didn't do would reflect well on me. I took responsibility for myself and let him do the same for himself. I lost a few old friends who were put off by my new priorities, but found a new and more heart–based relationship with both old and new friends who shared my values and perspective. However, this did not happen overnight, since it involved rebuilding on a new basis.

- **Values.** My parents had given up on their religious traditions by the time I was five or six years old, and instead had concentrated on financial success and social status. My father loved his work as a sales manager in business machines, and my mother was a homemaker and hostess with full time help.

I was given every material advantage, including private school education from seventh grade through four years of college. In a way, their approach to life helped me to see that material well–being and social status were not enough and to experience an inner longing for "more".

Before the crisis, I seemed to be caught in their value system and unable to act on my own unspoken values. After the crisis, I knew I had to put my own values into action as a matter of personal integrity and authenticity, both of which are necessary aspects of the spiritual life. Our energy becomes dissipated if we fail to live what Carl Rogers called congruent lives, being inwardly consistent and outwardly expressive of the persons we are.

More Consequences

Of course there is much more to the ongoing process of creative living than I am able to share on these few pages. This was only the beginning. In the weeks, months and years since the turning point, there have been and continue to be many healings, learnings, and crises of various kinds. However, a basic trust in the living process and the continuity of my soul provides a degree of confidence in meeting the many challenges with which life presents us. Following are a few more consequences I have experienced.

- **Healings.** One very important discovery I made in succeeding months was that I had a number of what I called "emotional sore spots" that blocked some areas of my being from trusting the inner spirit and the creative life process. It became apparent that these areas very much needed to be healed, and that healing might be a lifetime process of hurts and mendings. Many personal growth workshops and occasional sessions with therapists helped me along the way, as did close friends with whom I could have an open and trusting relationship, as they could with me.

- **Theology.** A few years after the crisis situation, I became involved in an evangelical Christian organization which placed primary importance on spiritual experience and the sharing of such experience with others. For a time, this affiliation provided an outlet for my new enthusiasm, but after several years I found that my open–ended and shifting views on the nature of God no longer fit within the association's acknowledged doctrines. One event in particular was the occasion of a moment of insight, which took me outside the approved boundaries. I was attending a conference at which a clergyman was once again, for the umpteenth time since I had known him, confessing his sin of lust for an attractive woman. I decided on the spot that there had to be a better way, a more creative way, to deal with such a problem than a series of confessions. I replaced the doctrine of original sin with what Matthew Fox called years later "Original Blessing", and came to see souls in distress as damaged rather than sinful. This was just one of many new perspectives, one which was affirmed by a statement by George Leonard in a talk he gave in 1966: "We have heard enough of the same sick old doctrine of Original Sin."

- **Callings.** In recent years many people have spoken and written of leaving high–powered careers in favor of more satisfying ways of life. Careers based on external goals and ideas of success that fail to honor a person's being can often lead to depression or worse. My problem was somewhat different, in that I was involved in activities that did not begin to enlist my best skills and talents. In either case, the problem is in failing to listen to the heart and honor the uniqueness of the soul. It took time, more education, and several changes of direction as I sought to find my way in mid–life – and it is a continuing challenge. Writers that are particularly helpful in this aspect of living from the soul are Parker J. Palmer (THE ACTIVE LIFE, LET YOUR LIFE SPEAK), Dawna Markova (I WILL NOT DIE AN UNLIVED LIFE), and Gregg Levoy (CALLINGS). Years ago, in his book TRUST, Jack Gibb spoke of one's "passionate path", which at least in my case has been anything but straight. It seems that a serious loss of energy is a sign that one has lost one's way and needs to do some inner listening.

•   **Community.** From a "normative" perspective, community is usually defined as a gathering of people residing in a particular location or of people coming together with a shared interest, activity, purpose or concern. From an "integrative" perspective, any of the above may be true, but the overriding bond is an open–minded, open–hearted, soul–connected sharing of life. The emphasis is on being real in relationships, with mutual listening, caring and sharing both joys and sorrows. In my own need, I created such a group late in 1957 with young mothers like myself who attended the same church at that time, and I have participated in many such groups in the intervening years. They have often served as family, especially for those of us who never had such open relationships in our families of origin. Even a community of as few as two or three members can make a great difference in quality of life.

•   **Altruism.** Many of us were brought up to believe that in order to be good persons, we should "deny" ourselves in order to serve others. However, if we are living in the creative, integrative mode, we care for ourselves *and* for others at the same time. Many Christians seem to forget that Jesus said to love our neighbors *as* ourselves, not *instead of* ourselves. Some writers have pointed out that in performing altruistic acts, we experience pleasure in return; it is not a one way street. In the 1960s Abraham Maslow wrote in TOWARD A PSYCHOLOGY OF BEING of such integration when he posed a question: "How could selfish hedonism be opposed to altruism when altruism became selfishly pleasurable?" However, altruistic acts can be a problem to both the giver and the receiver if the gifts are given as a *means* to self–worth rather than an *expression* of same. I came to realize that in this case we use persons out of our own need rather than respect them out of our own sense of being and self–worth.

Concluding Thoughts

What I have written in these few pages is only a beginning in exploring the many dimensions of the soul–connected, well–grounded spiritual life. There are so many books, tapes, lectures, seminars and workshops to help us on our way that we need not feel as isolated in our search as I did almost fifty years ago. The body/mind/heart/soul connection and oneness with the all are becoming common topics of discussion, at least in some circles, and hopefully will continue to spread. A few of the principles which I have found so import-ant in my own life:

- An ultimate trust in the Creative Spirit, both within ourselves and in all of life, which means letting go of other securities on which to base our lives;

- A continuing openness of both mind and heart for new learning and new experiencing, an open–system way of living;

- A willingness to revisit past and buried painful experiences to open them to healing love, finding new freedom and compassion for ourselves and others;

- A commitment to being who we are and giving our caring best to a world that desperately needs all we are and all we can be.

> *Are you in earnest? Seize this very minute –*
> *Boldness has genius, power and magic in it.*
> *Only engage, and then the mind grows heated –*
> *Begin it, and then the work will be completed.*

> **Johann Wolfgang von Goethe**

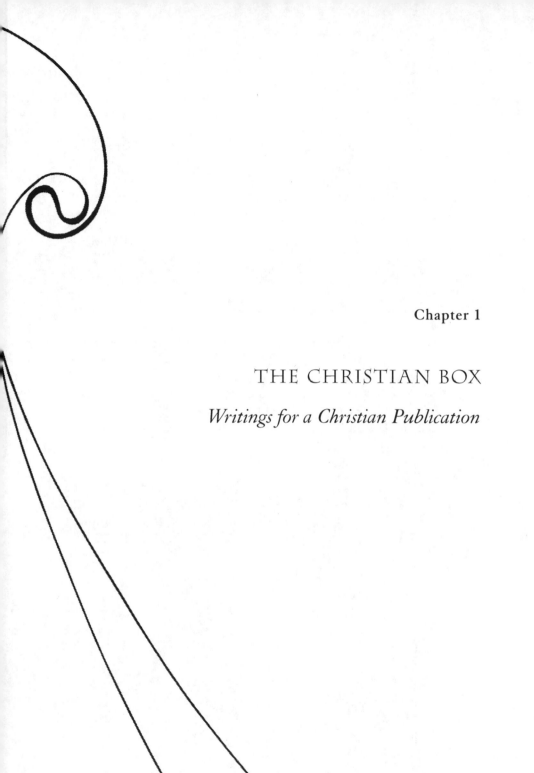

Chapter 1

THE CHRISTIAN BOX

Writings for a Christian Publication

The God who relates *authentically* is not some type of divine parent wishing to rescue wayward children. The divine–human relationship is not a co–dependent one; the relationship of the covenant is *adult–to–adult*, a model that is largely unknown to the formal religions.

Diarmuid O'Murchu
RELIGION IN EXILE,
A Spiritual Homecoming

The God I was told about in church, and still hear about from time to time, runs about like an anxious schoolmaster measuring people's behavior with a moral yardstick. But the God I know is the source of reality rather than morality, the source of what is than what ought to be. This does not mean that God has nothing to do with morality; morality and its consequences are built into the God–given structure of reality itself.

Parker J. Palmer
LET YOUR LIFE SPEAK,
Listening for the Voice of Vocation

*I*n the months following my "crisis of spirit" and breakthrough, I was a very enthusiastic Christian. I arose early each morning to read the Bible and other books of a spiritual nature, and I invited several of my good friends (young mothers like myself) who attended the same church to form a weekly prayer and Bible study group. The minister of our church strongly disapproved of our gathering, saying that it was "dangerous" for us to meet without his guidance, but we persisted without his help and discovered a wonderful time of sharing which would not have been possible had he been present.

Soon after the crisis experience, I was encouraged to enroll in a graduate course to study for a master's degree in Christian Education. At that time (1957), women were barred from ordination as clergy in our church, so the best I could do to "serve God" was to pursue the Christian education path. As a part–time, married student commuting from out of town, I was saved from having to live in a dormitory with the single women, and as a degree student, I took my theology courses at the seminary with the men. I rather enjoyed those mixed classes after six years in a girls' school and four years in a women's college.

One of my fellow students, a woman from Illinois, introduced me to a magazine and organization called FAITH AT WORK, an evangelical interdenominational group based in New York. In my new–found enthusiasm, I contacted the FAW folks and soon was invited to write an article for the December issue of the magazine. It was the beginning of a four or five year involvement with the organization, attending conferences on the East Coast, leading groups, and helping to initiate conferences on the West Coast.

Following is the first article I wrote for the magazine. I find it difficult to imagine, over forty years later, that I actually used such religion–based language as appears in the article. It surely indicates that I continued to think at that time within the Christian doctrinal paradigm.

The Journey

IT WAS CHRISTMAS EVE, FOUR years ago. Once again my voice was joined with those of the other members of the choir of the congregation in Charles Wesley's beautiful hymn of joy at the good news of Jesus' birth. "Mild He lays His glory by, Born that man no more may die; Born to raise the sons of earth, Born to give them second birth... Light and life to all He brings..."

The church, as always on Christmas Eve, was filled to overflowing. It was a handsome new church, with great wide chancel, giving an unobstructed view of the altar and the magnificent white–and–gold hangings so painstakingly executed by the Altar Guild. And as always on Christmas Eve, the choir was at its best. Light? Life? Second birth? Here in this glorious setting, such things were not hard to imagine. But what of everyday living?

Over the sink in our kitchen was a prayer card sent me many years before by my high school French teacher: "For the happiness of our earthly life; for peaceful homes and healthful days; for our powers of mind and body; for faithful friends; for the joy of loving and being loved: we thank Thee, O God." Several phrases of this prayer did not ring true for me, and I knew it.

Our home was anything but peaceful. It was frequently the scene of bickering, nagging and tears, and my husband seemed to be staying away from it as much as possible by throwing himself into his work and spending time with business associates. I in turn looked to community and church activities as a source of satisfaction, in the mistaken belief that this was the best contribution I could make to society. And both of us found escape in an all–too–busy social life.

I Had "Everything"

And yet I had "everything" according to conventional standards. I had a busy life, an education, good health, a handsome and successful husband, two fine children. But I was lonely! In spite of being surrounded by family and friends I had always been basically lonely. I had the uneasy feeling that the kind of love I was giving my husband and children was not the kind of love of which our Lord spoke, nor indeed had I ever experienced this kind of love in family relationships.

During the months prior to Christmas I had given considerable time and thought to the meaning and purpose of life. One by one I had set aside as invalid the various aims which the world seemed to consider worthwhile: education, material wealth, business prestige, social position, and even community service. None of these by itself offered a purpose for life, nor a means of establishing love and peace among individuals and nations. I became convinced that somehow the Christian faith could give the answer, even though I had not actually experienced the answer.

From Bad to Worse

After Christmas, matters went from bad to worse. In fear and desperation over my own inadequacy to meet even the basic requirements of the Ten Commandments, not to mention the Sermon on the Mount, and with our Lord's teaching on the sanctity and permanence of marriage pounding through my mind, I found myself, late one evening, on my knees before the altar of the church, talking to God in a way I had never done before.

Quite frankly I admitted to Him what a dreadful mess I had made of my life, and how inadequate was the love I had been able to give to those who were in any way dependent on me, and I begged Him to take over the direction of my life, whatever the cost might be. What I felt at that moment was a total willingness, at long last, to yield my life to God in a firm commitment. In spite of my willingness, this great step took more strength than I could muster, and so I asked God if He would take me over and "pull me through" the moment of decision.

And once it was all out in the open and clear in my own heart and mind, I suddenly knew that this was what He had been waiting for thirty–two years to hear from me. For the first time I was completely dependent on my Heavenly Father, and the joy and release that came as a result of this new relationship were immediate and almost unbelievable.

This experience was so extraordinary and so complete that I tried at once to express it to others, but unhappily I was unable to find another living soul in our church who seemed to understand what I was talking about. In a sense then, I made the "journey" alone – but I soon began to find "companions" in my hours of prayer and reading the Bible.

Suddenly the writers of the Gospels, and St. Paul, and even the Old Testament prophets came alive for me, and Charles F. Whiston, through his book "Teach Us To Pray," was of immeasurable help. Little by little I discovered other writers: Thomas Kelly, Fénélon, Evelyn Underhill, Austin Pardue, S. M. Shoemaker, E. Stanley Jones, Bryan Green, Norman Grubb, Eugenia Price – and of course, Faith at Work Magazine.

In terms of living human fellowship, that first year was a solitary one – and yet my loneliness was slowly but surely disappearing, and being replaced by the deepening awareness of God's love in the area of my family life. The new insights, which came to me through prayer and the study of the Gospel, led me to see that there could be no compromises. We had difficult problems to iron out, with some real conflicts, and some of these still exist; but the difference between the present and the past is the difference between night and day. There is a new peace, and an atmosphere of loving concern.

I am now able to give my children a whole–hearted and forgiving love, rather than a demanding one. At the same time, I can discipline them without my former feelings of guilt. I no longer feel a desperate need to get away when the going gets tough, and the children on their part feel a new security, which evidences itself clearly in their schoolwork and their relationships with other children. My husband and I are of different faiths, but even the problems of such a marriage are slowly being worked out in the light of God's love and our growing understanding.

Probably one of the most exciting aspects of the Christian life is the way God brings people to us who need his help—and who can help us. I was longing for the experience of Christian fellowship when a fellow member of my parish, the real estate saleswoman who had sold our house to us, came my way. She was the mother of two teen–agers and of a baby boy. I lent her a feeding table for the baby, and about a year later when she came to return it, I invited her in for a cup of tea. During the conversation that followed I told her how our family life had changed since I had given God His way in my life and she asked me many questions.

She took some books home to read and when I saw her at church the following Sunday, she was positively aglow. Actually, without saying a word about it, she had committed her own life to Christ during our conversation over teacups!

This friend and I then formed the nucleus of a prayer–study group for women, and at a time when the parish was in need both spiritually and financially, a number of us in the neighborhood applied for permission to start a new guild, one in which the primary emphasis would be on prayerful study of the Bible, in order that we ourselves might grow in Christian faith and commitment. We knew that only in this way would we be able to come to the point where we could successfully communicate this faith to others.

Something More Wonderful

We began to study the Bible as we had seen it done at parish life conferences — reading the passage, then sharing insights and discussing its application to our lives. We soon realized that in this small fellowship we had found something more wonderful than anything we had known in our church life up to this point. Slowly, in one person after another, the Christian Gospel became and is still becoming the one most important fact of life, and we have found under the guidance of the Holy Spirit and a real source of growth and strength.

We have not been without the problem of opposition, but for almost two years now we have continued to meet together, to serve the church according to our talents and to bring the Good News to others. We frequently welcome new members to the group and have already had to say goodbye to one old member whose husband was transferred to Salt Lake City, but we sent her off with a real sense of commission rather than tears of remorse.

Though I am an Episcopalian, I have found wonderful understanding and kinship in talking to the pastors of the Baptist and Presbyterian churches in our immediate area, something that could not have happened four years ago. It was, in fact, the Baptist minister who introduced me to Elton Trueblood's book, "Alternative to Futility," which our group has found most useful in helping to bring others to an understanding of the potential of the Christian faith.

These four years have been exciting. I feel that I am still on the threshold of new insights and experiences, and I can truly say, even after this comparatively short time, that the old defeated life is finished, and that I have a sense of what it means to be victorious in Christ.

My second article for Faith at Work appeared four years later and revealed some signs that I was beginning to move beyond the boundaries of the Christian box. By that time I had left my master's degree studies, having found that the "fellowship" among most (not all) of the faculty and students was based largely on commonly held beliefs and commonly performed rituals rather than on a deep and heart–felt sharing of life.

While I very much valued my courses in Old and New Testament and in Church History, I had also come to believe that truth in matters religious was just as temporary as in science or any other area of life. In fact, it was while reading a passage from Isaiah that I concluded that only an open mind could come to see even broader truths than those available in religious doctrine and dogma.

It was also at this time that I began to discover a kind of psychology that made much better sense to me than most of my undergraduate studies in the subject. My son, who was in fifth grade at the time, was having difficulties in school, and when I went to talk to the principal about his problems, he introduced me to Carl Rogers' book, *On Becoming a Person*. That was the beginning of my interest in humanistic psychology and such authors as Abraham Maslow, Clark Moustakas, Rollo May, Sidney Jourard, and Charlotte Buhler, an interest which has continued to the present time.

One additional experience contributed to my explorations beyond the boundaries of the Church. A friend invited me to attend the monthly meetings in Berkeley, California, of the Academy of Religion and Mental Health, a group consisting mostly of Christian psychiatrists and clergy. We were usually the only two women in attendance, and lay persons at that. The discussions were very interesting and we were welcomed as active participants. I eventually concluded however, that the psychiatrists were trying to fit the theology into their own conceptual framework and the clergy were trying to fit the psychology into theirs, without much success. Perhaps it did not occur to them that they would have to let go of their own positions in order to reach a new synthesis.

It was while I was in the midst of such new explorations that I wrote the following article.

Stages in Worship

MY INTRODUCTION TO THE WORD "worship" was at the age of three or four when my Sunday School teacher used it to indicate the time when we met together to sing hymns and say prayers before going to our classes. This early concept certainly tied worship to a specific place and a specific form of activity. Later, in the seventh grade, I began to attend another church where much time was given to acquainting us with the contents of a prayer book so that we could "actively participate in the worship of the church." My basic concept of worship remained much the same as the pre–school level, still tied to a specific place and even more tied to a specific form.

Through the ensuing twenty years and the experiences of college, marriage, and parenthood, I continued to accept the old concepts in most areas of my life without much thought or question, but with a growing sense of uneasiness. I became increasingly aware that all was not well within me and I began to search for deeper purpose and meaning for my life.

Sunday morning "worship" was at this point nearly meaningless for me, and God seemed very remote. Perhaps my deepest need was to feel loved just as I was, and when I was unable to find even one person who could accept me completely, I discovered the reality of God as an inexhaustible source of love and truth. And many life–long concepts began to change.

Among other things, I discovered that whatever we may say with our mouths at a church service, we do in fact worship that which we trust most completely for our own security, whether it be money or power or popularity or ability – or God. A friend once pointed out that as I learned to trust God, I found more and more freedom to "entrust" myself to people, and worship became a moment–by–moment living out of life of the love I was beginning to experience in this new relationship.

More and more I came to feel that the heart of worship lay in the reality of everyday life and that the Sunday morning service was true, meaningful, and creative only to the extent that it was spoken and shared expression of this life. The phrase "where two or three are gathered in my name" came to mean where two or three are gathered with a basic and personal trust in the living God and with openness toward one another. There could be no real worship where security was sought in denominational forms or theological viewpoints rather than in the Spirit of truth and love, nor where people were afraid to be honest about themselves with one another.

In recent months, my concept of worship has taken on a new dimension: the fulfilling to the utmost of the potential of the unique person God created me to be. It seems to me that most of us spend a lifetime trying to reach a goal or goals on the outside rather than living out our already existent potential from the inside —rather like acorns trying to become maple trees.

The result is not much of anything, neither oak nor maple, and hardly a glory to God in the fullest sense. How many of us ever stop long enough to discover our inner potential, and then have enough faith in God and His purpose for our lives to follow through without regard for financial security, family approval, or community status?

And how many of us discover and become free of the crippling emotional "sore spots", the hurts, fears, and guilt which inevitably afflict every human personality to some degree and which prevent us from being truly at peace with ourselves and therefore with our neighbors? We can often conceal these sore spots over a period of time, but in a crisis, when our security is threatened, they often erupt in fear, anger, and resentment.

Perhaps a measure of our worship of God is the extent to which we let these sore spots come to the surface and find healing to God's love, and in turn lead others to this same healing. We find new freedom to love ourselves, in the best sense, and in turn find new freedom to love others.

I wonder whether there is any higher expression of worship than the love in our hearts which gives to others the same freedom to be themselves which we find God gives to us, and then the openness of our minds through which God is able to broaden our concepts and lead us into an ever deeper understanding of His truth. And I wonder whether we can call our church services "worship" unless they are a means to and an expression of this deeper reality of God for each person present, a gathering together where group community and personal integrity are two sides of the same coin rather than a threat to each other, a corporate expression of the Spirit of truth and love through which each person becomes more truly himself and at the same time more at one with his neighbor.

We have a choice. We can say "Lord, Lord" or we can let God raise us to a whole new level of life where we do indeed worship Him "in Spirit and in Truth".

Chapter 2

INSPIRATION

A Letter in Response to an Inspirational Book

. . . true self will come to our rescue, if we let it. The divided life is pathological, so it always gives rise to symptoms – and if we acknowledge the symptoms, we may be able to treat the disease. In my case, the symptoms became impossible to ignore.

Parker J. Palmer,
A HIDDEN WHOLENESS:
The Journey toward an Undivided Life

. . . we are told that the voice of inner knowing is not real. When we fear the power of the life force, we become stuck in the dull round of conventional responses. "Something lacking!" The frozen state of apathy, conformism, and confusion is normative, but must not be taken as normal.

Stephen Nachmanovitch,
FREE PLAY:
The Power of Improvisation in Life and the Arts

Personal power is exactly what it sounds like. It comes from within. It's a person allowing his or her authentic self to define his or her life. Personal power is creative power.

Cliff Havener,
MEANING:
The Secret of Being Alive

*I*n 1964 I came across a book entitled THE TRANSPARENT SELF by Sidney Jourard. This book stirred me to the core, so much so that I wrote a letter to the author to share my excitement at what he had written. My letter was forwarded to Sid in England, where he was meeting with R. D. Laing about psychological issues of interest to them both. It was the beginning of a correspondence which I have recorded in full in another book, but for our purpose here my first letter is sufficient.

At about the same time that I wrote this letter, a number of women in our small communities in Northern California became inspired to share what they had been learning about human consciousness and caring. One friend told several of us of her vision of opening a lending library where we would make our books available to other women (and men if they were interested) and where books could be ordered for purchase. We enthusiastically supported her vision, and thus the Lodestar Library came into being.

We located a delightful small brick building with leaded glass windows and door, set well back from the street in the center of town. Over the main room was a small attic (reached by an external staircase) that served as a business office and a setting for one–to–one conversations. In addition to taking turns being available for signing out books, we also welcomed talking with our customers and offering suggestions as to which authors might be suitable in response to their concerns. The library functioned for several years, until public libraries and commercial bookstores began carrying the same materials.

At about the same time that the Lodestar Library came into being, another group of women came together to found the Seasons of Life Forum. Authors of books we had found meaningful were invited to speak at the Forum every month or six weeks. When I learned that Sid Jourard would be giving a seminar at the Esalen Institute on the West Coast in mid–November, and that we had no speaker invited for that time, I suggested his name to the board of directors of the Forum. The suggestion was eagerly accepted and *an invitation extended. The evening was a great success, and I welcomed the opportunity to meet Sid Jourard in person.*

My initial letter to him follows.

September 28, 1964

Dear Dr. Jourard,

I'm only as far as chapter 12 in THE TRANSPARENT SELF, but am so excited about what I have already read that I can hardly stand it! Several other books have affected me in a similar way and I have always meant to write to the authors (like Victor Frankl, Carl Rogers, Jacob Bronowski and others) but have never gotten around to it.

To give you a little background, let me say that I am 39 years old, married, and the mother of 14–year–old girl and a 12–year–old boy. My husband and I could be exhibit A for some of the problems you state in chapter 6. I received my B. A. in psychology from Smith College in 1946, probably the only student to graduate in that field without taking the course in abnormal psych. My grades were not outstanding, my only A's having been in the introductory course and in a senior year seminar in social/experimental psychology, both with Fritz Heider, and probably more in response to Mr. Heider than to the material. Do you by any chance know where he is now?

In any case, I had no inclination to go on to graduate school, perhaps for two reasons. First of all, I couldn't see that all the psychological insights, valid though they might be, had much practical effect on the lives of the members of the department, and the suicide of my professor of mental measurements and testing the day after the final exam only confirmed my opinion. Secondly, my own emotional needs were such that I was far more interested in marrying a man who would (I thought) love me without telling me what to do. Poor boy, he was as much under a delusion in this area as I was!

Ten years and two children later, things were a mess and I was desperate. In the light of my convictions, I wasn't about to go to a psychiatrist, and I soon discovered that my close friend and rector of the church in which I was very active (ugh!) was in even worse shape than I was and totally unable to help. There seemed only one other possibility, and that was God. So in prayer I asked a Spirit in whom I had no more reason to trust than that I believed intellectually that He existed and that He was truth and love, to take over the direction of my life. Amazingly enough, it worked. I don't mean that one day I was a mess and the next day I was whole. But life started to go in a completely new direction, and the integration of the system began to take place that you describe at the beginning of chapter 9. I was no longer pulled in fifty different directions by trying to please people and undertake many responsibilities in order to feel that I was worth something. Action began to be an *expression* of an inner sense of worth and integrity rather than a *means* to trying to find such a sense – and I could say "no" to people without feeling guilty! Also, it wasn't long before I began to realize that being true to the direction of this Spirit was always in accord with being true to my own real "self" – not a case of "self–sacrifice".

Another interesting development was an intensely felt need to be as much as possible the same person on the outside that I was on the inside, in order not to misrepresent myself to people. At first I think this was pretty much a moralistic kind of thing: if I were going to be true to God, I would have to be truthful, period. But I soon discovered that there was a spiritual law involved, and a much better reason for being open, namely that it actually took a kind of energy *not* to be myself, and that this energy could far better be spent in creative ways. Ignoring this spiritual law seemed to mean spiritual death in much the same way that ignoring certain physical laws can mean physical death. And then of course I made the exciting discovery of how dynamic a relationship can be between two people who are at least approaching being their real selves.

Shortly after the turning point in my life (1957), I began to attend classes at the local Episcopal seminary and women's training school, with the idea of getting a master's degree in Christian education. It seemed to me that the church was missing the point. But before long certain problems developed in my schooling! Among other things,

I have a deep inner need to be logical (strange bedfellow with this tendency toward mysticism, don't you think?), and I couldn't see that the human mind would have been any better able to know the whole *spiritual* truth 2,000 years ago than it was able to know the whole *scientific* truth. So I decided that for me all religious doctrine and dogma would have to be tentative, subject to change with new understanding just as scientific concepts are subject to change – and with that decision, my religious concepts began to change so fast it made my head swim. I finally quit school, but not before taking a course in Liturgics in which we were required to write a critical analysis of the proposed revision of the Communion service in the Book of Common Prayer. Are you at all familiar with this? One of my suggestions was to replace the Old English word "comfortable" with the word "inspiriting" – and I meant by it the same kind of thing you describe in chapter 9, even though I was coming at it from the theological end. Anyway, it seems to me that the closer we come to truth, the less need there is to separate it into different "fields". Basically, it's all one.

Time out to finish the book – which has only served to raise a few more exciting issues which are food for thought and discussion. But I have no more time to write, which I do slowly. Let me just add a couple of more points: 1.Having *ultimate* faith in this healing, creative Life within me (which to me is an aspect of God's nature) seems rather practical, since I can take it with me and it doesn't finally depend on outward variables; 2. While I'm seldom sick now, I can almost always recognize the "dispiriting" conditions which bring on any sickness and can see why the sickness is very convenient; 3. Over the last couple of years, through greater sensitivity to my own emotions and sometimes with the help of another person, I've been able to locate several emotional "sore spots" which were causing me to react at the childish level rather than from the inner consciousness of self–acceptance; 4. Dissemblance seems almost a God–given protection to the real self when, as children, we are emotionally dependent on persons who are unable to accept us as we are – but it becomes so much a part of us that we fail to recognize when it is no longer necessary and in fact is a hindrance to our survival as persons; 5.The most dispiriting factor in my own life right now is my failure to live up to my own potential as a human being, either emotionally or intellectually – and somewhere there's an answer I haven't seen yet. Like maybe go back to school?

Well, I can't help but think along with Teilhard de Chardin that this world of ours is on the verge of a whole new level of life where your prophecy on page 152 will come true, and much more besides. It's a thrilling prospect, even though things look like such a mess at the moment.

Thanks for listening (if you've been able to last this long!), and please let me know if you ever have reason to come to California. We have a guest room ready and waiting, and there are many of us here who would love to meet and get to know you – your real self, that is! And thanks, too, for writing the book.

"Faith–fully" yours,

In November 1965, following a weekend seminar at Esalen when Sid was the featured speaker and which I attended, he did indeed travel to Walnut Creek to speak at our Forum. His talk was an unqualified success, and while he was not our houseguest, I did have some time with him when I drove him to San Francisco following his talk. A comment he made during that drive that I "seemed to be a spirited wench" had a definite effect on my self–awareness and led to further correspondence and occasional personal contact in the years following, until his accidental and most untimely death at age forty–nine.

Chapter 3

NEW VISTAS

Challenges in Returning to Formal Education

We need to create an environment in which learning makes sense and occurs within a context that gives it meaning. Many teachers all over the country are making valiant attempts in this direction, but it is a difficult change to implement because it implies a radical paradigm shift with far—reaching consequences for our entire way of life.

> Alfonso Montuori and
> Isabella Conti:
> FROM POWER TO PARTNERSHIP:
> Creating the Future of Love, Work, and Community

The firmest foundation of all our knowledge is the community of truth itself. This community can never offer us ultimate certainty – not because the process is flawed but because certainty is beyond the grasp of finite hearts and minds.

> Parker J. Palmer,
> THE COURAGE TO TEACH
> Exploring the Inner Landscape of a Teacher's Life

All of us have a gift, a calling of our own whose exercise is high delight, even if we must sweat and suffer to meet its high demands. That calling reaches out to find a real and useful place in the world, a task that is not waste or pretense. If only that life—giving impulse might be liberated and made the whole energy of our daily work, if only we were given the chance to be *in* our work with the whole force of our personality, mind and body, heart and soul . . . what a power would be released into the world! A force more richly transformative than all the might of industrial technology.

> Theodore Roszak,
> PERSON/PLANET:
> The Creative Disintegration of Industrial Society

*I*n July of 1966 I filed for divorce from a nice person who was married to his career and was not interested in any kind of counseling which could have improved our relationship. I recognized at that point that I would have to go to graduate school in order to support myself in any kind of professional work.

In preparation for graduate school, I signed up in the spring of 1967 for two courses at our community college. One was in Statistics and Probability, which I would likely need in graduate study, and the other was loosely related to Great Books. The Statistics teacher was a godsend, not only very good at explaining concepts, but offering open book exams with all the time we needed to complete them. I also had the opportunity to study with two young men in the class, which was very helpful. Under such ideal circumstances, I did very well in the course.

The concept which I best remember from the course has to do with probability. I was fascinated by the idea that there could be different odds on the same event (such as tossing a coin), depending on whether it was viewed a single event or part of a series. Both/and, not either/or. My first recollection of such a concept was in a college physics course (1943) on the theory of light, in which the wave/particle theory is both/and, not either/or.

As for the Great Books class, it was my first experience with written assignments since my undergraduate years more than twenty years earlier. I had disliked writing papers to such an extent that I had vowed never to go back to school, but this time I rather looked forward to the opportunity because I felt I now had something to say. The following article was one of my assignments for this course, a somewhat different take on both/and than in math and science.

Both/and

When Man not merely knows, but experiences in his emotional nature that the union of contrasts is his destiny, he is saved, no matter how hideous his history and despite the vast indifference of the older generations. A new generation that rejoices in the union of contrasts must take over and make itself heard.

Lancelot Law Whyte

ONE OF THE LITTLE PLEASURES of life is to come across a statement by an author or philosopher which affirms the discoveries we are making in our own life experience. Such a pleasure was mine when I read an editorial in the Saturday Review (November 12, 1966) by Lancelot Law Whyte, British author, lecturer, and philosopher. The above quotation consists of the last two sentences of the editorial and expresses both the general sense and the specific primary point of Mr. Whyte's thoughts.

More and more I have come to feel that life is not so much an either/ or proposition, as I had once supposed, but rather a matter of both/and, the union of contrasts of which Mr. Whyte speaks. Perhaps one of the greatest steps forward that humanity will take will be in the discovery that form and feeling, purpose and passion, direction and desire, spirit and senses are in fact complementary parts of the whole rather than conflicting forces, and that the strength of neither part need be diminished in order to function effectively in the total picture. Alan Watts (Beyond Theology: The Art of Godmanship) states at least a portion of the problem rather colorfully:

Spirituality needs a beer and a loud burp, just as sensuality needs a bed on the hard ground, a rough blanket, and a long look at the utterly improbable stars.

In reading <u>Civilization and Its Discontents</u> I wanted to call out to Sigmund Freud that man indeed may find a way out of his dilemma. Perhaps we are just beginning to realize that we have been wearing blinders and thus seeing only a part of the whole, and a solution will become possible only as we become aware of more and more of the factors involved in the total problem.

Freud, in confronting the question of the "oceanic" feeling of his friend and its possible religious connotations, is at least able to allow for the possibility of the co–existence of what he calls "this primary ego–feeling" with "the narrow and more sharply demarcated ego–feeling of maturity" in the mental life of many people, but it apparently never occurs to him that <u>both</u> feelings — the sense of oneness with the universe plus the unique definition of the individual may in fact be essential to the full and mature functioning of the human being.

It is apparent that some people, like Freud's friend, are aware of the "oceanic" feeling at the conscious level, while others, if they have it at all, are certainly not aware of it. As for myself, for many years I was aware of an inner hunger for something I could not find, and it was only at the age of thirty–two, in the midst of a personal crisis, I first experienced this oceanic feeling at the conscious level. In a desperate situation, I gave myself over to whomever or whatever I believed God to be — an all–loving, all–accepting Consciousness — and in the process discovered not only a new sense of oneness with all of nature, but began to know myself in a completely new way as a unique individual with a sense of worth simply because I existed rather than because I was living up to some ego–ideal. I began to find a new freedom to be myself rather than what I thought I <u>ought</u> to be or what others expected me to be. This new basis of orientation has persisted and somehow has diminished or done away with an old fear of "not–being".

There remains the question of why some people experience the oceanic feeling while others do not. It is conceivable to me that we are cut off from an awareness of the feeling in early childhood to the extent that we are made to feel guilty about our "natural" selves and to view our libidinal drives as "bad" and "not us". Or perhaps we lose contact with this inner sense of "eternity" in being taught to strive for an ego–ideal rather than to live out an already existent "potential person" much as an acorn becomes an oak tree. It is possible that in our growing human awareness of others, we seek too often to be <u>like</u> others or to possess what others have, and in the process not only deny our own unique potential, but become frustrated to the point of aggressiveness in attempting to accomplish the impossible, something which is contrary to our true nature. This is of course assuming that we have a true nature, a real self, a premise which some people might deny.

Freud raises the question of the purpose of life, and in rejecting a religious concept of such a purpose, turns instead to an attempt at deducing a purpose from an assessment of the actual behavior of men. He comes up with the pleasure principle, the positive aim of experiencing strong feelings of pleasure and the negative aim of avoiding pain. But perhaps this is another area in which we human beings are missing the boat simply because we are failing to see the total picture. By this time we should know that total avoidance of pain and suffering is impossible and be ready to experiment with more creative ways of dealing with it, such as accepting it rather than attempting to avoid it. By this I certainly do not mean a masochistic attitude of going out and looking for it, but rather a realistic acceptance of what comes to us in the course of life. I have become convinced that if our total personality is growing and maturing, we can be far more resilient in the midst of pain and suffering than we may yet realize.

Freud points out that we are threatened with suffering from three directions 1. our own body; 2. the external world; and 3. our relations to other persons. This is true, but it seems that we often compound our suffering with a fear of suffering. And it is also possible that those who, like Freud's friend, have experienced the oceanic feeling of oneness of all life, may in fact be better able to accept pain as a part of the totality of the life on this earth. Freud states: "We are so made that we can derive intense enjoyment only from a contrast and very little from a state of things." I cannot say whether this is wholly true, but I do know that I would rather experience both joy and suffering intensely than know only the shallows of human emotions. I would rather love deeply and take a chance on being hurt than never love at all, or love half heartedly. "The happiness of quietness" no doubt serves a purpose in life, in fact has served a purpose in my own, but I find it cannot compare to the sense of vitality which comes with embracing all of life.

As for the "employment of the displacements of libido" as a way to personal peace and fulfillment, I somehow feel that I am interested only in displacement. I like Bertrand Russell's assessment of the problem in Marriage and Morals:

The animal and spiritual natures should not be at war. There is nothing in either that is incompatible with the other, and neither can reach its full fruition except in union with the other.

It is with considerable relief that I am finding this to be so in my own experience.

I suspect that a key issue in the whole problem is the way we see and interpret aggression. If we understand it as a basic human drive, then I can foresee no possible solution to our dilemma, but only a mounting sense of frustration under the increasing controls of civilization, and an accompanying breakdown in the human emotional system .

But if we see aggression simply as an outgrowth of fear at all levels of life, then perhaps we have a chance of finding a way out of our distressing situation. As little by little we discover the various means of diminishing fears at both the physical and psychological levels, we may come to realize that aggression becomes less and less of a problem. It is true that the number and extent of our fears may seem overwhelming, especially in the psychological area of fear of not–being and fear of rejection by others, but perhaps the oceanic feelings of people like Freud's "religious" friend will have more to contribute to the resolution of our conflicts than we have thus far anticipated.

For myself, I cannot find satisfaction in an illusion, nor in attempting to escape from reality, in intellectualizing all my feelings, or solely in the enjoyment of beauty. I find Freud's verdict that "the program of becoming happy cannot be fulfilled" to be inadequate and will continue to search for a broader answer which will encompass the total human being, not a partial answer through regulation but a total answer through integration. I do not accept the idea that our enemy in the struggle is "the human instinct of aggression and self–destruction", but rather that it is a deadly sense of inertia in the midst of our confusion and feelings of futility.

As Freud says, man is becoming more Godlike, "but does not feel happy in his godlike character". If man should discover, however, that becoming Godlike means not denial but enhancement of his deepest instincts, and that these instincts are after all a good and necessary part of the whole, he may see his growing "Godmanship" (to steal a word from Alan Watts) in an entirely new light.

He may discover, too, that at the heart of the Christian myth, disguised though it may be by irrelevancies and half–truths, is a "saving" truth to the effect that "love fulfilled", or Agape, is stronger than Death, and that Eros and Agape are complementary forces which together create a total life.

I conclude in the words of Lancelot Law Whyte:

This redemption from excessive conflict, this state of grace (fulfilling the Christian hope and surpassing the self–dedication of Marxists and Freudians to their partial doctrines), this enjoyment of the unity beneath all contrasts, this vital understanding blending mysticism and logic and flowing into action and creation, is the meaning of Man—what he is here for—a state transcending science plus love. Certainly it is our only hope.

Methuselah

At the same time that I was enrolled in the community college courses, I read a notice in our local paper announcing a unique summer program to be offered at the University of California at Santa Cruz, a coastal area dear to my heart. I had visited the campus briefly in January 1967 and considered it beautiful beyond compare. Admission to the program (Methuselah), which was to be a community of adults of all ages (children also welcome), would be based on a letter of intent explaining the applicant's reasons for choosing to participate.

With my divorce to become final early that July, I decided that opting for this once–in–a–lifetime opportunity, which in fact it turned out to be, would be a most desirable bridge between my old life and the new. I wrote my letter of intent, was accepted with a tuition grant (my funds were very limited), and thus came to experience one of the best summers of my life, both intellectually and socially. My son (15) was with me the latter part of the summer, and my daughter (17) visited on week–ends.

Some of those who enrolled in the program commuted to the campus from the local area, while many of us lived in the Cowell College dorms. We attended seminars in Cowell College classrooms, all situated among towering redwoods. We listened to lectures and participated in discussions with outstanding scholars from all over the country (with no exams!).We took our meals in the glass–walled college dining hall, inspired by magnificent vistas out over pastures, often including cattle, to the ever changing waters of Monterey Bay. We spent lazy afternoon hours at the Cowell swimming pool or nearby state beaches and redwood forests.

Although we had been told that there would be no exams or written assignments, the professor of philosophy did ask us to write a paper on one of the existentialists we were studying. I hesitate to include it because it is so academic in nature, but if you find it boring, you can skip over it. It served a purpose in pointing out to me that some teachers don't want students using one discipline to explain another. I made the mistake of addressing a philosophical problem with psychological insight – something which I did not then and do not now consider a mistake!

(Untitled Essay)

In the light of Walter Kaufmann's comments in his introduction to EXIS-TENTIALISM FROM DOSTOEVSKY TO SARTRE, I rather hesitate to point out what for me are rather serious deficiencies in Sartre's lecture on EXISTENTIALISM. Kaufmann says of the lecture (p.45): "It contains un-necessary misstatements of fact as well as careless and untenable arguments and a definition of existentialism which has been repudiated by Jaspers and Heidegger, and ought to be repudiated by Sartre, too, because it is no less unfair to his own thought". This leaves me with the uneasy feeling that I may be beating on air, which would surely be a waste of time. I hope that not all of what follows will be a meaningless waving of the arms.

Sartre makes quite clear what he means when, in speaking of atheistic existentialism, he says that existence precedes essence: "We mean that man first of all exists, encounters himself, surges up in the world and defines himself afterwards. Thus there is no human nature, because there is no God to have a conception of it." But in my opinion, this is rather like saying that there is no science of physics because there is no God to have a conception of it. What has that to do with the matter? If he were to say instead that there is no human nature as defined in the story of the Fall because for him no Old Testament God exists to thus define it well, that would be something else again. But even so, he fails to take cognizance of the fact that all con-cepts are human concepts, including the concept of God, and that human concepts do change. In fact, it seems to me that he ignores the whole area of conceptualization as though it does not exist and has no effect on a (per-son's) choices in a situation.

Sartre says (p.306), "It is true in a sense that we do not believe in progress. Progress implies amelioration; but man is always the same, facing a situation which is always changing, and choice remains always a choice in the situ-ation". This apparently is Sartre's own life experience, but it is not mine. I agree with R. D. Laing (THE POLITICS OF EXPERIENCE, p.99) that "As we experience the world, so we act. We conduct ourselves in the light of our view of what is the case and what is not the case". And Sartre's view simply does not fit my experience.

To say that a transcendent spirit does not exist simply because we reject the Old Testament concept of God is rather like saying that a particular phenomenon in scientific research does not exist because it does not act as we at first thought it acted. It seems to me that Sartre rules out all possibility of experiencing a transcendent spirit by assuming at the outset that there is no such spirit. I can make no such assumption, nor can I rule out the possibility of progress.

In contrasting the two states of "being–for–itself' and "being–in–itself", and in defining "being–in–itself " as a rigid "external" model, Sartre seems to leave out a third possibility which might be called "being–of–itself". This possibility I conceive as a state of reflection when a new awareness of understanding of the experience of being–for–itself becomes possible. A wider and more inclusive or corrected concept then permits one to return to the dynamic state of being–for–itself, with the potential of a broader experiencing because of a broader range of vision. Being–of–itself must be seen as a growing framework, subject always to correction and expansion, and not as a permanent, static form of security. Santayana's traveler would exemplify the point in question.

To put it another way, Sartre seems to say that there is no Eden to lose and that we are starting from confusion, without allowing for the possibility of degrees of confusion. For myself, the myth of Eden is certainly not a position to which we return, a paradise to be regained, but rather a step in our growth of awareness. Of course there is seeming confusion when new experience and awareness ("knowledge", if you will) comes into conflict with old patterns of understanding, but it seems to me that the solution then is to go beyond Eden. For me, there is no need to throw out Eden as never having had meaning, nor to return to Eden as the end–all of life. The point is rather to discover or create a new "garden", but one which will be seen only as a temporary resting point, an oasis for refreshment, before setting out again into new territory, exploring new possibilities.

To return to the question of essence and Sartre's concept of essence as man's definition of himself as he exists and makes choices in the midst of the life situation, I find that for myself, I must be open to the possibility of a pre–existent undefined essence, a continuum out of which I discover or create —or both — my own "variability" or unique definition or particular essence. From this point of view, the "self" is perceived as a differentiation of essence, much as stained glass or a prism differentiates the light which passes through it. But the stained glass or prism would itself be in process rather than static.

Constant choosing out of essence reveals ever–changing patterns of color, but patterns which are true to the uniqueness of the person.

In a way, this is close to what Clark Moustakas (CREATIVITY AND CONFORMITY, p. 26) describes as creativity:

> Many times in my life I have been faced with a dilemma that, after much struggle and deliberation, turned out to be illusory. I continually discovered that in authenticity, I discover my unique self.

Thus the example which Sartre cites of the young man who is confronted with the choice of whether to stay with his aging mother or to go off to fight in a war which for him has personal meaning would present itself to me as rather a different problem.

First of all, I would be concerned with making a choice which would affirm my own sense of self, and secondly I would not be able to assume in advance that my aging mother would have no further cause to live if I were to depart. I would have to assume that she has a choice as to how she will respond to my decision, just as I claim this freedom of choice for myself. My concept of love is apparently different from Sartre's, in that love between two people necessarily includes a freedom to act and respond without assuming in advance that the other will not have the same freedom. It is a mistaken concept of love as manipulating, controlling, and needing to fulfill the wishes of the other — denial of freedom of choice — which leads to self– and other–imprisonment.

> I have hesitated to include the professor's comments on my paper, but have decided that some of you may be interested. The question marks in parentheses indicate words which I could not make out in the hand–written comments.

Your points are clearly made and reasonable enough as an indication of why you find (it seems) little in Sartre. From his standpoint things are somewhat different, I'd say. He is not really interested in a particular view of God. In fact, for him — and he says this — it would make no difference to his position if God exists. The Sartrean world starts with the absence of God and tries to draw the consequences of that absence. The problem of essence only begins with humanism; it ends with a conception of phenomena in their immediate (?), i.e. their "originary" character. From this point he moves on to an examination of the fundamental nature of the "Being" of man — an ontology of human existence. The level of concern is then below or fundamental to the actual events of existence. The polarities of being for–itself and being in–itself are grounds for human action, not ways of describing men in action. You seem, as I read you, to (?) Sartre's descriptions as a psychology of Man, but his concern is with the conditions which make individual action possible. He approaches those conditions by way of a theory of consciousness (but not a psychology of consciousness). In brief his targets are in another sphere.

With good wishes,

M.N.

As for the over–all message, I did indeed understand Sartre's stance, but I happen to believe that a valid theory incorporates information from all relevant disciplines. Even more than that, I passionately believe that crossing the boundaries between academic disciplines, health professions, religious beliefs, nations and cultures is essential to creative solutions to our many personal, social, political and environmental problems. Our planet and its people are hurting badly, and healing can only happen when we remove the blinders which confine us to our narrow perspectives.

Chapter 4

MORE CHALLENGES

Graduate School Term Paper

Humanity is . . . faced with an urgent challenge of unparalleled magnitude. Specifically, rigidity in the generative order, to which control through rewards and punishments makes a major contribution, prevents the free play of thought and the free movement of awareness and attention. This leads to false play which ultimately brings about a pervasive destructiveness while at the same time blocking natural creativity of human beings.

David Bohm and **F. David Peat,**
SCIENCE, ORDER, AND CREATIVITY

The evidence is good that we are now in the midst of a paradigm shift of major proportion and significance. We are being challenged from all around us to make profound leaps in who we are and how we understand. Trusted truths are not only failing to provide answers, they often prove inadequate even for understanding the questions.

Charles M. Johnston,
THE CREATIVE IMPERATIVE,
A Four–Dimensional Theory of Human Growth &
Planetary Evolution

*F*ollowing the magical summer in the natural setting of redwoods, mountains and sea, the social environment of a diverse gathering of participants of a wide range of ages and backgrounds, and the intellectual challenge of stimulating lectures and discussions, I returned home to prepare for a major life change. My next step would involve not only entry into graduate studies, but leaving behind my children, my friends, and my home of many years.

Thus it was that in early September of 1967, I packed up as many of my belongings as seemed feasible and, with a friend of many years, began the long drive across the country to Toronto, Canada. Leaving my children, ages seventeen and fifteen, in California with their father proved much more painful than I had anticipated. I wept for the first half hour of the trip and on numerous subsequent occasions. At the same time, I was experiencing the excitement of new challenges: a new course of study, a new city and country, an apartment of my own (a first), and a possible new relationship with a man who would eventually become my partner in marriage.

The first few months were exceptionally, but probably not surprisingly, difficult. I broke out in a rash on my arms and for the first time in my life took sleeping pills. In time, I made new friends and adjusted to life as a graduate student in Educational Theory at the Ontario Institute for Studies in Education (University of Toronto). I flew to California for the Christmas holiday and stayed with a dear long-time friend, since I was not welcome to stay in my former home with my ex-husband and his parents. My children were welcome in my friend's home and were able to spend a considerable amount of time with me.

On returning to school, I decided against continuing in the Department of Applied Psychology, where my studies were so much a repeat of my undergraduate work and where there was little of the collegial atmosphere I had experienced during the previous summer. Fortunately, the head of the department understood my complaints and my wish to transfer to the Department of Adult Education, but I was not permitted to transfer until the end of the school year.

Before my departure from the Applied Psychology department, I was enrolled in a course which was required because I had taken no education courses as an undergraduate. The professor lectured the first half of the class time and encouraged the students to give presentations during the second half for extra credit. Most students spoke about a particular learning theorist, but I chose to talk about the implications of humanistic psychology for education. It was new subject matter for all present and proved to stimulate the liveliest discussions of the whole course. I very much enjoyed myself, and when I went to the professor's office several weeks later to retrieve a paper I had written on creativity in education (unfortunately I can't find the paper), he said he had understood my presentation better than one he had heard just the previous week on the same topic at Harvard. With that kind of praise, I left the department with good feelings.

My second year proved to be an exceptionally satisfying experience, as I became a member of a community of professors, students, and staff. As graduate assistant to my advisor, I sat in for him in a course on Individual Learning, and also received course credit for reading extensively on the topic of creativity. In a course on Psychology of Adults, I asked permission to write a term paper in my own way and on my chosen topic, and was encouraged to do so. That paper appears here just as I wrote it, although I later updated some of the terminology, mostly relating to gender. It was the only assigned paper I ever wrote which received an A+, with glowing comments.

Growth Of Conciousness

P R E F A C E

It was in the garden of a madhouse that I met a youth
with a face, pale and lovely, and full of wonder.
And I sat beside him on the bench, and I said
"Why are you here?"
And he looked at me in astonishment and he said, "It is
An unseemly question, yet I will answer you. ...
Each (father, mother, teacher) would have me but a
reflection of his own face in the mirror.
Therefore I came to this place. I found it more sane
here. At least I can be myself."
Then all of a sudden he turned to me and he said,
"But, tell me, were you also driven to this place by
education and good counsel?" And I answered, "No, I am
a visitor."
Then he said, "Oh, you are one of those who live in the
Madhouse on the other side of the wall!".

Kahlil Gibran[1]

IT WAS A LONG AND dreary fall, those last months of 1956. I felt rather like a clock that had nearly run down, with no one to rewind it. My marriage was little more than a superficial relationship, and my many social and community activities had long since begun to pall, leaving a void which nothing else seemed to fill. At one time those activities had appeared to give me some sense of worth and purpose to my life or to me as a person, but now they were only pressures pulling me in too many directions, leaving me empty and exhausted.

Stripped of those activities, I found nothing at the center of me except perhaps an anxiety as to whether life had any purpose at all. And if not, why bother? My religious faith, which I had considered to be strong and secure, deteriorated to the point where God seemed either remote or non-existent.

My need to find some meaningful solution to the combined problems of external pressures and internal nothingness eventually reached crisis proportions and brought me to that moment of truth when I discovered that I had been trying to play the game both ways, with two opposing sets of rules. I had attempted to be what others expected of me in order to gain their acceptance, but at the same time had continued the struggle to be myself, even though I was still quite unaware of who that self was.

In that moment of crisis, without really knowing consciously what I was doing or what the implications might be, I chose to be myself no matter what the consequences, and it was the beginning of a whole new life. I experienced myself and the world about me with an intensity I would not have believed possible, as though seeing all for the first time, and I felt amazingly close to or even a part of all of nature. I seemed to have lost much of my fear of "not being," and to have gained a capacity to see relatedness in much that formerly seemed unrelated. This new sense of integration, both within myself and with the rest of creation, was especially exciting. I began to see and relate to people in a wholly new way.

I know now, many years later, that it is not simply a matter of choosing once and for all to be myself, but rather that I must make this choice over and over again in many different situations if I am to continue to grow into new life. I do not always have the wisdom or the courage to make this choice, but when I make it, I can count on deeper relationships, increased understanding, and greater fulfillment of my abilities as a unique human being; I am no longer a run-down clock needing to be re-wound, but an electric clock plugged in to the source of energy.

Part I: The Great Split / The Greater Whole

In general, in our early months and years,
we were amongst the active contributors to
what was going on wherever we happened to be.
We were open to experience and ready to
participate in what was taking place. We lived
our lives from the inside out. Whatever we
did was an expression of something we really
cared about or a reaching out to something
which attracted us. We related actively and
directly to people (and to things) and if we
were lucky the other people in our lives did
the same to us.

D.M. MacLeod[1]

A TWO–WEEK OLD BABY CRIES in his crib, and we assume that he must have a need for food or dry diapers or to be held or just to cry. It would never occur to us to disbelieve him, to question his integrity. We assume that his outward behaviour corresponds directly to his inward state.

This child has not yet learned the art of dissemblance. He is not yet sufficiently conscious of the world around him or of himself as a separate entity to act in any way except spontaneously according to his present need. He has not yet discovered the conflict which can result when he seeks to meet two of his greatest needs, the need to maintain and extend his own integrated self, and the need to gain the love and acceptance of others. He is still in touch with his own feelings, and they are acceptable. Thus far, no one has rejected him for being himself. He is still "turned on" as he was at birth, and still communicating his true feelings without any attempt at deception.

With the passing of time, our baby grows in awareness of himself and of the world about him, and hopefully is still quite spontaneous in his interaction with the fascinating environment of people, places, and things. Hopefully, he will be restrained from this spontaneous interaction only when he is endangering his own well–being or that of others. But if his experience is like that of most of us, he soon runs into opposition from those closest to him when he freely expresses his thoughts and feelings. He begins to suspect that there is something wrong with him, that he is somehow "bad," for expressing anger or wanting his own toy or exploring his own or another child's body. He is led to believe that "nice children" do not take toys away from other children or play doctor or keep the biggest cookies from themselves – or do many of the things which are a natural expression of maintaining or furthering their own existence as individuals and of exploring the world about them in order to relate to and enjoy it to the fullest.

Our child is not simply restrained from actually hurting himself or others, but is made to feel unacceptable because of his natural need to be in touch with himself and the world about him. Any aggression or destructiveness on his part is interpreted as a basic badness which needs to be punished and controlled rather than as a secondary reaction to the frustration of his primary potentialities. More and more often he finds that he has to choose between 1) being honest about himself and with others, and 2) gaining the approval of others at the expense of his own integrity. The natural in him must be denied if he is to be acceptable to his parents, teachers, and the society of which he finds himself a part. If he is a member of a family with an orthodox religious orientation, he may find the threat of a disapproving, life–denying god added to all the other pressures. "The Great Split" between the inner reality and the outward formality is well under way, and continues on into adolescence and adult life.

> We have shown that man is not necessarily evil but becomes evil only if the proper conditions for his growth and development are lacking. The evil has no independent existence of its own, it is the absence of the good, the result of the failure to realize life.
>
> Erich Fromm[2]

(The adolescent) is thrust back upon himself. The insistent natural press within him toward becoming whole is met perpetually by unbudging resistance. Schools, rooted as they are in a Victorian century and seemingly suspicious of life itself, are his natural enemies. They don't help as they might, to make that bridge between his private and the social worlds; they insist, instead, upon their separation. Indeed, family, community, and school all combine – especially in the suburbs – to isolate and 'protect' him from the adventure, risk, and participation he needs; the same energies that relate him at this crucial point to nature result in a kind of exile from the social environment.

Peter Marin[3]

This not–so–mythical child of ours and the adult he is becoming must find some way of functioning in a culture of group conforming, life denying pressures, and it appears that several ways are open to him. The way or ways he adopts are not likely to be a conscious choice, but will be determined (at least in the early stages of his life) by his own temperament and by the kind of relationships to which he is exposed. These ways are 1) image–fulfillment, 2) image–smashing, and 3) self–fulfillment, and while a person probably functions in each of these ways at different times and in different aspects of his life, his general approach to life is likely to be dominated by just one of them.

There is a fourth way, but it is in fact no way at all and falls outside the present discussion. It is the way of non–entity, the way of the human being who is able to find identity neither through the image adopted by a particular segment of society nor through the realization of himself as a unique person. He could hardly be said to exist at all.

The way of image–fulfillment requires putting all one's effort into maintaining the image which is expected of one, whether by parents, the church, the educational system, or the particular community or culture of which one is a part, or more likely by a combination of these. The person internalizes this composite image and makes it his own, and in the process must deny or repress his natural inclinations (whether thoughts, feelings, or actions) which would be in conflict with the acceptable image. Unfortunately, what he gains by this method of functioning is not *self*–acceptance but *image*–acceptance, and he lives with an unconscious anxiety which can never be satisfied until or unless he discovers the life–giving release of self–acceptance. He flees his unrecognized anxiety in many ways, through seeking hoped–for security in such things as affluence, political power, or social status, or through diversion in travel, entertainment, or even education and career, or perhaps through oblivion in alcohol, drugs, or sex if he can manage this without destroying the image.

The life of the image–fulfiller is full of "oughts" both for himself and for others. His behavior is largely based on an externally–determined value system which he perceives as ultimate authority, whether expressed through particular persons or institutions or both, and he is likely to assume that others should accept this same ultimate authority even though they have not chosen to make it their own. He feels responsible *not* for making his *own* decisions but for making decisions acceptable to that authority, and often for seeing to it that others do likewise. Since he has to repress many of his own natural feelings in order to maintain his image, he is unable to identify with the natural feelings of others, but rather is judgmental with them as he is with himself. He is more likely to feel *responsible for* others than *responsive to* them, with a need to control them instead of allowing them to take responsibility for themselves.

> "Love lets the other be, but with affection and concern. Violence attempts to constrain the other's freedom, to force him to act in the way we desire, but with ultimate lack of concern, with indifference to the other's own existence or destiny. We are effectively destroying ourselves by violence masquerading as love."
> R. D. Laing

Our image–fulfiller is in fact both a product and a begetter of a kind of violence which may appear to be loving concern. His own freedom and integrity have been violated in such a way that he cannot admit to a unique existence or destiny either for himself or for others. His fear of and anxiety about himself makes him fearful of and anxious about others, so that while in the very act of professing love for another person, he may be attempting to manipulate that person to satisfy his own anxieties.

For the image–fulfiller, other significant persons in his life are seen as extensions of his own image and means to improving his view of himself, not as unique individuals to be respected and related to in their own right. He chooses friends who affirm his values and who fill out in the desired way his picture of himself, either through affiliation, submission, or domination. He sees a spouse or a child as someone to be conformed to his own image, and will become anxious at evidence of rebellion against or non–conformity with this image. He is not really sure of himself, since he does not in fact possess himself but possesses only an image which is not his own, so he is in constant need of re–confirmation of his image by the other significant persons in his life.

Marriage between two image–fulfillers may be tolerable and even in some measure satisfying, but it will never be the spontaneous, ever–renewed union which is possible between two persons who are growing towards real personhood. There is always a measure of violence in a marriage based on image–fulfillment, in that each partner must to some extent deny the other as a person in order to maintain his own self–view. And a real crisis may be expected if one partner begins to discover the meaning of becoming a person while the other continues to hide in fear behind the image. Soon they will speak a different language.

The image–fulfiller's energy is likely to be exhausted in two directions: outwardly, in maintaining the image and preventing evidence of the real self from breaking into the open (public relations work), and inwardly, in holding together the conflicting elements in the image itself, since it is probably formed from various sources not all congruent with each other, and holding together in some way the image and the real self. Little or no energy remains for creative output, nor is there sufficient acceptance of the natural self and its life–energy to make extensive creativity possible. That very self which has been denied and repressed is the source of creative energy. In today's terms, the image–fulfiller is "up tight!"

The second way of approaching life, which is in fact the other side of the coin of image–fulfillment and which may be considered a kind of image–fulfill-ment of its own, is the way of image–smashing. The person who follows this way senses enough of the natural self within him to know that the role of con-formist is not for him, and yet he fails to sense or experience enough of his real self to trust that self either as a center from which to perceive the world around him or as a base from which to take action.

The image–smasher's energy is largely expended in rebelling against those who set up the requirements which would make him acceptable to them – the "Establishment" in whatever form or forms it imposes itself upon him. His actions are directed towards proving that he is not and will not be the way "they" want him to be. He has no "oughts" either for himself or oth-ers except for the ought of rebelling, and he has no ultimate values except perhaps the value of being value–less, i.e. rejecting the values of his culture.

Unlike the image–fulfiller, the image–smasher does acknowledge his own thoughts and feelings, but since he has no more of an integrated sense of self than has the image–fulfiller, these thoughts and feelings find expression in a largely disintegrated way and contribute to a general sense of helplessness and hostility. He seeks power *outside* himself by rebelling *against* rather than *within* himself by building *for* – through destruction rather than creation – and in the process may destroy a little more of himself.

> To be nobody but yourself in a world which is doing its best, night and day, to make you everybody else – means to fight the hardest battle which any human being can fight, and never stop fighting.
>
> e. e. cummings[5]

He refuses to recognize external authority in society, but neither has he discovered the internal authority of the integrated self. If he accepts any authority at all, it is probably the authority of his emotions and the emotions of others like himself. He neither accepts responsibility for himself nor is capable of any great responsiveness to others, and his world is likely to be one of anarchy and chaos.

The image–smasher represents what the image–fulfiller most fears he will become if he should let go of his conformity and control. But what each fails to see is that both are victims of the same depersonalization, with one as tied to maintaining the image and submitting to and exerting controls as the other is to smashing the image and lashing out against controls. Neither one is a free man, responsible for himself and responsive to others. Each has known the violence of manipulation and/or indifference in his formative years, and each expresses the violence which has been done to himself in his

> We can never be born enough. We are human beings; for whom birth is a supremely welcome mystery, the mystery of growing: the mystery that happens only and whenever we are faithful to ourselves.
>
> e. e. cummings[5]

relationships with others, either through control or rejection. The one retreats to rationalization and form while the other retreats to emotionalization and feeling. Neither one knows wholeness. Neither one knows himself.

The third way is the way of self–fulfillment or self–actualization or self–realization, the way of freedom which is directly opposed to the bondage of image–fulfilling or image–smashing. It is the way of the person who is fortunate enough not to have to make the choice between being himself and gaining the love and acceptance of others. Or it is the way of the person who discovers that, while such a choice may once have been necessary to maintain his existence in the face of pressures which he was too vulnerable and immature to handle, it is now possible to be true to himself and at the same time to find acceptance from others who are discovering the same freedom. He either escapes or resolves the Great Split.

The self–fulfiller has no "oughts" either for himself or others in terms of externally or culturally imposed value systems, but he knows that freedom of inner values and direction which comes with love of self and of others. And he trusts in the capacity of others for this same inner direction. Because of this basic trust which frees him of the need for dependence or domination, he can enter more deeply into human relationships and open himself more freely to new experience.

Since his sense of worth lies more in himself as a person than in the approval of others of his actions, relieving him of the need to control or be controlled by others, he has a greater freedom to experiment with life, to explore new ways of doing things, and to be interdependent with others in the sense of allowing his legitimate physical and emotional needs to be met.

The self–fulfiller finds satisfaction not in competing against and defeating others, but rather in making the most of his own uniqueness. He knows that he is the only person alive with his particular combination of talents and motivations, and his aim is to fulfill this uniqueness to the utmost. He is likely to see himself as complementing other persons rather than as in competition with them, and finds his sense of well–being in discovering and making the most of his own potential rather than in driving his way to the top of some common heap where conformity rather than uniqueness is the ideal. He is more concerned with being true to his own pattern and color than with trying to make others seem colorless.

> "There is a vitality, a life-force, an energy, a quickening which is translated through you into action, and because there is only one of you in all time, this expression is unique. And if you block it, it will never exist through any other medium and be lost. The world will not have it."
>
> Martha Graham[7]

Because he is integrated and therefore sees and experiences all aspects of his being as contributing to his total self rather than as in conflict with each other, the self–fulfiller's energy can go into expressing that whole rather than into dealing with conflict. As a result, he comes through to people in Technicolor. In today's terms, he is both "turned on" and "tuned in", and he rejoices when others find this same quality of life for themselves. He knows that when others come through in Technicolor, expressing their own special patterns, they do not compete with him but rather enhance his own being.

In our present society are abundant examples of the image–fulfillers, the image–smashers, and the self–fulfillers, and of all degrees in between these extremes.

On the educational scene, the patterns are particularly evident. Some students are still conforming to the status quo, putting all their efforts into obtaining high grades on the performance of tasks set for them by external authority, tasks which involve little more than memorizing or assimilating information and for which they would likely find little motivation if external pressures were removed. For those students, creative approaches to personally meaningful problems are not a common experience. Because they fit well into existing structures, they are not likely to embarrass the authorities with their questions or actions. They live up to what is expected of them.

Today's student activists, on the other hand, seem to be divided between the image–smashers and the self–fulfillers, between those who advocate destroying the existing institutions at any cost (with methods up to and including violence) and who have little to suggest as to a better way of operating, and those who, while objecting to the present state of affairs, are directing most of their energy into exploring and experimenting with new and hopefully more creative ways of functioning. The former are burning down buildings and destroying computers, while the latter are starting experimental schools and trying out new methods for encouraging personal growth.

Similar contrasts are apparent in all areas of society, and it remains to be seen which path the majority of us will eventually follow. Will we continue to try to live up to an image which we believe, rightly or wrongly, that society requires of us, or will we find increasing courage to be our true selves and thus the capacity to grow to new levels of being?

> "When I say that self-disclosure is a means by which one achieves personality health, I mean something like the following: It is not until I am my real self and I act my real self that my real self is in a position to grow. One's self grows from the consequence of being."
>
> - Sidney Jourard[8]

Part II: Both Essence And Existence

"Dark and cold we may be, but this
is no winter now. The frozen misery
of centuries breaks, cracks, begins to move,
the thunder is the thunder of the floes,
the thaw, the flood, the upstart spring.
Thank God our time is now when wrong
comes up to face us everywhere,
never to leave us till we take
the longest stride of soul men ever took.
Affairs are now soul size.
The enterprise
is exploration into God
where no nation's foot has ever trodden yet."

Christopher Fry[1]

SEVERAL HUNDRED MILLION YEARS AGO a fish adapted to the hazards of nature in rather an amazing way by developing lungs in addition to gills. Thus, when the waters receded, he was able to exist in the dry mud for as long as several years, until the waters returned. His existence during this dry period was somewhat like a bear's hibernation. So successful was this adaptation that the lungfish, as he is called, can still be found in a few places today in essentially the same form as he took on millions of years ago. But is he really much better off than before developing his lungs? What is it worth to be "stuck in the mud?"

The lungfish had a cousin, on the other hand, who developed legs as well as lungs and crawled off across the land to new freedom. This cousin no longer exists, but he became the means through which a higher form of life evolved. His was an open–ended road rather than a blind alley.

"You know what I think? I think you're emerging just to get away from me."[2]

For some time now I have felt, along with many others, that we human beings are in the midst of a transition every bit as crucial as that of our fishy forbears, and that much of the emotional distress which we find within us and around us is in fact an indication of the struggle involved in such a transition. We may be discovering, however, that the static environment of receding and returning waters which made the lungfish's adjustment possible is not even open to us, and that a rapidly changing environment is forcing us to "emerge" or perish.

As we look back over the history of man's growth, it is apparent that the solidarity of the group of which he was a part was essential to his physical and psychological safety. It was in conforming to the group beliefs and customs that he found his own identity and security. Various outlets and/or controls were provided for handling his aggression and hostility, and as codes of laws were developed to ensure the continuing functioning of the group, he obeyed out of fear of punishment.

For a particular stage of man's growth, this identity through group conformity seems to have been an appropriate means to his security and well–being. His level of consciousness has been such that he has not yet been aware of his own psychological needs which when unmet have resulted in destructive behavior, and so the system of laws and punishments has persisted as a solution for restraining him from harmful actions. He has not yet been sufficiently aware of himself as a unique individual to find his identity other than in the group, and so he has been quite willing to be a conformist in order to have a sense of being in belonging.

But a serious problem arises when, because of a man's growing awareness of himself and his environment, the beliefs and customs of the group or groups with which he has identified no longer correspond to his experienced needs. If for example a Christian begins to experience himself *not* as being basically "sinful," but rather as having very legitimate needs which call for fulfillment and fears which demand relief, then the doctrine of his church begins to lose meaning for him. Forgiveness of sins, which once assuaged his guilt for a self which he perceived as "bad" rather than "needy," is no solution to his problem as he now understands it. He is no longer seeking release

> *How can we speak of joy on this dark and suffering planet?*
> *How can we speak of anything else? We have heard enough*
> *despair. We have heard enough clever restatement of the*
> *same sick old doctrine of Original Sin. Those who dismay*
> *at humanity's condition have had their turn upon the stage.*
> *They have offered intricate critiques, sinuous analyses of*
> *everything that is wrong with mankind, leaving unanswered*
> *only the questions they have almost forgotten how to ask:*

from guilt for the "sinfulness" of his destructive behavior and of himself as a person, but rather for ways and means of growing beyond that destructive behavior through self–realization.

> *What do we do now? How do we change it all? How do we act to make our society and ourselves whole? At a time when at last we have all the means at hand to end war, poverty and racial insanity, the prophets of despair discover no vision large enough to lead men to the merely possible."*
>
> George Leonard[3]

*I*n much of today's world (particularly the West), man is struggling with just such problems as this matter of moving out of inadequate group identity into more adequate – and open–ended – self–identity. He is not as hungry as he used to be, and he has more time to explore his own thoughts and feelings and to consider the meaning and purpose of his life. He is no longer satisfied with simply conforming to the customs and accepting the ready–made explanations of existing institutions. In short, he is showing signs of abandoning image–fulfillment in favor of self–fulfillment, and those who still find their identity and security in the conforming society are filled with anxiety at these signs of what they believe will lead to chaos. Since they are not yet at home with their own inner selves, they cannot understand the freedom without license of the man who is. Their consciousness is still of the outside of things, while our new man has discovered the within of things, including himself and other human beings. While the image–fulfill-ers still see only outward behavior, and judge accordingly, our new man re-lates to the inward need and realizes that as inner fears and anxieties for the safety of the self find relief, destructive behavior decreases.

> *Kairos, a joyful and awesome moment in mankind's long day. Kairos. history ufolding like a bursting star. The present opening upon itself so that every scientist may becom a seer, every academic a prophet. kairos. A time when ten thousand voices in a multitude of strange tongues struggle to utter a single tought: The atom's soul is nothing but energy. Spirit blazes in the dullest clay. The life of every man – the heart of it – is pure and holy joy.*
>
> George Leonard[4]

This new man has not just suddenly appeared on the current scene, but has broken through here and there for hundreds of years. He has been, however, the exception – an occasional indication of the growing potential of the human race. Perhaps the infrequency of his appearance was a luxury we could once afford, but the time seems to be upon us when this new man must come into being in ever–increasing numbers if we are to experience the *breakthrough* rather than the *breakdown* of the human race.

It is only this kind of man who, because he has come to accept himself as he is and with this self–acceptance find the freedom to grow, is able to resolve so many of the apparent contradictions which are a source of conflict in so many human beings. He lives at a new level of awareness where he knows that form and feeling, purpose and passion, direction and desire, spirit and senses are in fact complementary parts of the whole rather than conflicting forces, and that the strength of neither part need be, nor indeed *may* be diminished in an effectively functioning whole. He be diminished in an effectively functioning whole. He knows that it is the relatedness of all aspects of life, and the acceptance of this relatedness, that makes growth to new levels possible.

For this man, there is no conflict between the Essential Life (or energy plus consciousness) which is the source of his being and through which he experiences a mystical oneness with the universe, and the Existential Form through which he experiences himself as a unique person, a particular expression of that Life. Each dimension enhances the other, making possible a whole which is far greater than the sum of the parts.

And for him there is no struggle to be a part of some in–group in order to feel secure, except for the in–group of the human race itself. His identity is not in being a French–Canadian or a Rotarian or an Eton graduate or a Communist, but rather in being human, and therefore he relates to others in the uniqueness of their self–identity rather than in the sameness of group identity. His concern for all human beings is not that we be "normal" in the sense of fitting unobtrusively into the existing landscape of society or of defeating each other in a common competitive game, but rather that each of us becomes all that he is capable of becoming.

> *Spirituality needs a beer and a loud burp, just as sensuality needs a bed on the hard groundd, a rough blanket, and a long look at the utterly improbable stars.*
>
> Alan Watts[5]

The question, then, is whether we can learn something from the story of the lungfish and his cousin as we seek to find solutions to our present solutions to our present human predicament enviroment. Do we choose to adjust to our present environment and continue to exist as painlessly as possible within it – an option which may not be open to us anyway since we ourselves have created for ourselves a rapidly changing environment – or are we ready to risk the probability of growing pains in order to transcend our environment and go on to a new level of freedom, awareness, and vitality? Do we want to hold on to the security of the status quo, which like the womb has served a purpose but in time has become not only confining but suffocating, or are we ready to accept as our basis of orientation the very dynamic of Life itself?

> *When Man not merely knows, but experiences in his emotional nature that the union of contrasts is his destiny, he is saved, no matter how hideous his history and despite the vast indifference of the older generations. A new generation that rehoices in the union of contrasts must take over and make itself heard.*
>
> Lancelot Law White[6]

We would do well to take another look at the so–called evidences of "break–down" in our society – school drop–outs, professional drop–outs, social drop–outs, marriage drop–outs, psychiatric drop–outs. Perhaps the school drop–outs, for example, have begun to feel in their bones the possibility of growing legs and walking off into a new land, but so far have seen only a "televised view" of this land through their own intuitive awareness

> *Indeed it may be the 'sick' of our society who introduce new values to living through the need to discover meaningful relationships at a depth level.*
>
> R. G. Howlett[7]

and/or the effect of such drugs as LSD. These young people may sense that the present educational system seldom provides either a conducive environment or suitable procedures for growing legs. But so far most of them have been unable to discover either an improved setting or new and more appropriate methods of exercise. They are not so fortunate as one young art professor I knew who, after being introduced to LSD by some of her friends and discovering through it a remarkable experience of reality and love, was told to forget about drugs and to go out and find the same thing through personal relationships in depth.

What happens to a man and wife or a parent of a child when one person wants only group acceptance and the security of a static environment while the other begins to discover the excitement of inner growth which comes with the often risky exploration and experiencing of new areas of life? Soon the two are no longer speaking the same language, and the one who has begun to explore new territory and discover new capacities is not likely to re–enter willingly the old confines of dark waters or dried mud.

Nor can we in good conscience urge such a return. This present time cries out for the discovery of new paths to growth and wholeness, a new integration of life at all levels. It is to be hoped that with the aid of our increasing consciousness, and an awareness of the destructive part that fear can play in clouding our vision, we may be able to grow legs as well as lungs, and thus walk off into a greatly expanded level of being.

Cosmic Dance

(April 1965)

The Star of Truth gives of himself:
A brilliance shimmering in random rays of infinite pattern,
a gleam penetrating the darkness of the ages,
finding release in expanding form.
In the fullness of time, the mind of Man opens to the Star
and perceives the golden symphony of revelation
with steps at first faltering, tentative, discretely variable,
yet moving always towards the continuous variability of the One.

The Rose of Love gives of herself:
A radiance embracing the particular in the midst of the all,
a glow melting the frozenness of the ages,
finding fulfillment in giving birth to life.
In the fullness of time, the heart of Man enters into the Rose,
and receives the crimson fragrance of tenderness
with steps at first fearful, hesitant, discreetly cautious,
yet unfolding always towards the passionate abandon of the One.

Crimson Rose and golden Star,
radiant love and brilliant truth,
the dance of Life and Form,
all One
In the consummate joy of Creation.

References

Preface

1. Gibran, Kahlil, "The Mad Man", <u>The Wanderer</u>. New York: Alfred A. Knopf, 1923, pp. 42 f.

Part I

1. MacLeod, D.M., A way of thinking about things in general and ourselves in particular. Unpublished paper, Toronto (16 Aldenham Cresc.), 1968.

2. Fromm, Erich, <u>Man for Himself</u>. Greenwich, Conn.: Fawcett Publications, 1965, p. 220.

3. Marin, Peter, The open truth and fiery vehemence of youth, <u>The Center Magazine</u>, 1969, Vol. 2, No. 1, p. 64.

4. Laing, R.D. as quoted by Mark Sheean in Newsletter One, Pacific High School, Palo Alto, Calif., an insert in <u>This Magazine is about Schools</u>, 1969, Vol. 3, No. 1.

5. cummings, e. e., as quoted in <u>To Be Nobody Else</u> by John Pearson. San Francisco: Jomeri Publications.

6. Ibid.

7. Graham, Martha, as quoted in <u>Art and the Intellect</u> by Harold Taylor. New York: Museum of Modern Art, 1960, p. 22.

8. Jourard, Sidney, Healthy personality and self–disclosure, in <u>Readings in Human Development</u>, Bernard, H.W., & Huckins, W.C. (Eds.). Boston: Allyn and Bacon, 1967, pp. 440–441.

Part II

1. Fry, Christopher, <u>A Sleep of Prisoners</u>.

2. Reproduced from <u>Saturday Review</u>, July 1, 1967, p. 49.

3. Leonard, George, from a statement made on behalf of the Esalen Institute to introduce a talk by Abraham Maslow at Grace Cathedral (San Fransisco), January 6, 1966.

4. Ibid.

5. Watts, Alan, <u>Beyond Theology: The Art of Godmanship</u>. New York: Random House, 1964, p. 1962.

6. Whyte, L.L., Man's task: a union of contrasts. Guest editorial in <u>Saturday Review</u>, November 12, 1966, p. 32.

7. Howlett, R. G., Hidden Springs: a therapeutic community. Unpublished paper, 1967.

Chapter 5

A HUMAN PSYCHOLOGY

Writings in a Psychology Newsletter

The reader will understand that we are here undertaking a fresh look at what it means to study the human experience. This fresh look puts greater emphasis on experience than on behavior, on meaning than on causality, on self–realization than on other–manipulation.

James F. T. Bugental, Ed.,
CHALLENGES OF HUMANISTIC PSYCHOLOGY

. . . in obedience to the rights of the person, I propose that we reverse the course of the cultural river, so that it flows out from the inherent needs of the person into the structures of society – on the assumption that the human personality is the most precious resource of all, one which enriches the entire species and ennobles the planet.

The choice I speak of is a new human identity, neither individualistic nor collectivistic. And for this we need a politics that has outgrown the modern infatuation with science and industrial necessity, a radi-calism that opens itself to the spiritual dimension of life.

Theodore Roszak,
PERSON/PLANET,
The Creative Disintegration of Industrial Society

$\mathcal{D}$uring the fall/winter/spring of 1966–1967, I had usually spent two weekends a month at Bridge Mountain, a growth center in the Santa Cruz mountains near Ben Lomond, California. My divorce had not yet been finalized, and this gave my husband the opportunity to spend time in the family home with our teen–agers. On one of those week–ends someone gave me a copy (Spring 1966) of the Journal of the American Association for Humanistic Psychology, as it was then called. I was especially interested in an article by Charles Tart on "The Bridge Mountain Community: An Evolving Pattern for Human Growth". On perusing the table of contents, I now note that the author of another article, James B. Klee, would become one of my professors during the summer of 1967 at the University of California–Santa Cruz.

I was already familiar with the writings of many of the members of the Association, such as Carl Rogers and Sidney Jourard, and decided that I would become a member of the Association myself. In a recent frenzy of cleaning out files, I came across my acceptance letter from the executive director at that time, John Levy. I have continued my membership for almost forty years.

The following fall, soon after my arrival in Toronto, I found a most wonderful book, CHALLENGES OF HUMANISTIC PSYCHOLOGY, edited by James F. T. Bugental. At times I continue to turn to this treasury of the writings of many of the founders of the Association for Humanistic Psychology (as it is now called). In subsequent years I became involved in the workings of AHP, attending and giving presentations at Annual Meetings, serving as a temporary staff member, and on the Board of Directors. Over a period of several years, I contributed articles to the newsletter, AHP Perspective, and on one occasion served as guest editor on the theme of creativity. Following are a number of articles which appeared in print during this time.

A Psychology of Creativity

(AHP Perspective, June 1986)

Something is happening in the universe. Whether or not we think of ourselves as creative beings, we are part of an act of creation that is continually taking place. To the extent that we consciously take part in this cosmogenesis, our lives are full; to the extent that we refuse to express it through creative activity, inhibited either by our own fears or by what we perceive to be repression from without, we experience pain and dislocation.

Lois B. Robbins,
WAKING UP! IN THE AGE OF CREATIVITY

THE GOOD NEWS: Life is creative process, and our life purpose is to be active participants in the process.

THE BAD NEWS: We human beings, in our fear and ignorance, spend much of our lives blocking the process.

PEOPLE OFTEN THINK OF CREATIVITY as solely the domain of artists who produce works of art as evidence of their creativity. We have begun to realize that the same principles which lead to the release of creative energy in artistic work apply as well to all other areas of life and relationships. To the extent that we participate in creative process and establish conditions which encourage others to participate in it, we affirm life; whenever we block the process in and between ourselves, others, and the environment, we violate life.

If we accept that each of us is intended to be a unique expression of creative process, then we can see that our life calling is to promote that process in whatever ways are appropriate to our own skills, experience and concerns. We also need to recognize that, when we block or undermine the process in our children, we are contributing to the formation of violated human beings who, unless they participate in effective therapy, will express this violation in some form of destructiveness either against themselves or against others.

Within this frame of reference, what we call "evil" is the consequence of unacknowledged, unhealed hurt/anger/hatred resulting from the violation of personal and interpersonal creative process and of the self–alienation which accompanies this violation. Children who have been violated in this way close off their emotional vulnerability as an escape from unbearable pain and as a means to self–preservation. They cease to grow emotionally and become prime candidates for criminal behavior. As adult criminals, each harboring the soul (and often the mind) of a battered child, they rape others as they themselves have been raped.

Creative process is healing, development and transformation. Healing is the process at work repairing and redeeming damage that has been done; development is the process at work fulfilling the potential of what can be; transformation is the process at work moving into new form when the limits of old form have been reached.

We have already learned much about the principles upon which creative process is based in human interaction – such as self–consistence, respect for self and others, openness to new information (from within and without), trust, spontaneity and tolerance for ambiguity – and we have much more to learn if we are to be effective participants in creative process in all areas of life.

We also need to recognize that the difference between good and bad family relations, education, religion, management, employment, government, human services, professional consulting, and so on, is the difference between the enhancement and the blocking of creative process.

As Patricia Mische observes in *Star Wars and the State of Our Souls*, the real battle is not between communism and capitalism, but between the mechanistic/divisive and the organic/healing (creative process) world views. Until we resolve this conflict within our own souls and come into the experience of oneness with our planet and universe, we will be unable to deal effectively with our human and environmental problems.

For centuries some among us have moved beyond alienation into lives of creative process in which living persons have been valued above dead ideologies and in which a sense of connectedness to others has replaced a need to control others – what Fran Peavey has called "heart politics." These people have given us dreams and visions of what our world can be, but we continue to insist on bypassing their process, attempting to bring those visions to reality by enforcement from a position of alienation. The process cannot be bypassed if we are to bring about deep healing and spiritual oneness.

I believe that it is possible that a theory of creativity will become as important to the human sciences as Einstein's Theory of Relativity is to the physical sciences. The question is whether we are willing to turn our backs on the gods of the mechanistic mode – material wealth, social status, intellectual superiority, restrictive religion, political one–upmanship, the arms race – as our primary means of power. Are we willing to embrace instead the universal power of creative process from which most of us have been separated since early childhood? If we are indeed willing, then our task is to learn all we can about the principles of creativity which appear to be the morality of the universe, the Tao, and to commit ourselves to their incorporation in our lives. We may thus become contributors to, rather than blockers of, the cosmic creative process of which we are both part and expression – a practical, challenging, meaningful and inspiring life journey.

. . . call it spiritual or mystic or aesthetic, or creative, or simply (humans) being (human), I am speaking about unknown forces in (humans) merging with unknown forces in the universe and letting happen what will, permitting reality to emerge in its fullest sense and letting the unpredictable in oneself encounter the unpredictable in the other. Then a break-through of self occurs in which (one) does the unexpected and emerges newly born, perceiving, sensing, and experiencing in a totally different way.

Clark Moustakas,
Creativity and Conformity

Personal Growth / Political Action

(AHP Perspective, January 1987)

IN RECENT YEARS, A NUMBER of people have declared the human potential movement – the search for personal growth – to be in direct opposition to effective social change. The search for self which Peter Marin called "the new narcissism" has been described as a dangerous block to or distraction from the political action that can bring about necessary changes in our ailing society. Many concerned citizens continue to argue whether there should be a relationship between personal growth and political action, and if so, what kind. Are the two in fact antithetical, or are they as inseparable as yin and yang? Are they totally unrelated?

Having been a part of one political scene or another (using the broadest definition of "political") for approximately fifty years, I have come to believe that who we are as persons has inevitable political consequences, although we occasionally express ourselves by our absence. Inaction, as well as total involvement of one kind or another, can be interpreted as a political act.

If this is so, the question is not whether personal growth and political action are related, but rather what their relationship is, what it should be in a democratic society.

Since personal growth is a lifelong process, finding ways of developing and fulfilling our potential as effective human beings will necessarily go hand in hand with expressing ourselves politically in the world around us. If the results of political activism are to be of a creative and long–standing nature, I believe that certain aspects of personal growth must precede that activism.

For many of us, growing up requires that we become self–alienated manipulators to survive psychologically in a world of adult power. To gain the acceptance and nurturance of those on whom we are dependent for many years, we learn to deny our own perceptions and see things as others want us to see them. We may also learn to deny any feelings that others find uncomfortable. In this process of self–alienation, we become displaced persons, losing touch with the natural creative energy of the universe as we lose touch with ourselves.

To involve ourselves in deliberate political action before we take the time to re–own ourselves and regain at least some measure of our authenticity is destructive for several reasons. For one thing, when we are out of touch with the natural creative power available to us when we express who we truly are, we tend to search in neurotic and manipulative ways for an alternative sense of power. We may pursue admirable goals with methods that fail to respect the worth and integrity of people who stand in our way.

Furthermore, when we seek security in anything less than the natural creative energy available to us all, we may distort our perception to justify and maintain our false security bases. We have to protect those persons or things we see as the sources or at least the safeguards of our power. Manipulating our power, we may do things *to* people (as though they were objects) in the name of social change rather than interact creatively *with* willing participants to find new and better solutions to our problems.

Entering into deliberate political action without taking time to recognize our own abilities and values also lessens our contribution to society. We will be operating on two cylinders rather than four and yet spending more energy in the process. Gaining self–knowledge is a life–long endeavor, and we do well to begin developing it as early as possible to make effective use of our social being.

If we accept the idea that personal growth and political action do in fact belong together, we must be aware that our common commitment to the concepts and processes of personal growth does not mean that we are going to think and behave alike politically on all the issues that confront us. We base our actions on whatever degree of insight we may have at any particular point in our lives rather than on what others think we should be doing. Because we are all in process, this will necessarily lead to political differences among even the most open–minded. To the extent that we are integrated, in touch with the life within us, we will discover a natural rhythm rather than an artificial balance based on someone else's calculations.

A balanced society is not one in which everyone does the same thing at the same time in the same way – fifty hours a week for personal growth, fifty hours for political action, fifty hours for sleep, etc. – but one in which each person can be deeply involved in whatever is right for him or her at any particular time.

"Holoself" versus "Higher Self"

(AHP Perspective, July 1988)

ON A NUMBER OF OCCASIONS I have found myself reacting against the use of the term "higher self", and since the term seems to be used ever more frequently, my reactions are becoming ever more numerous. The phrase, which was once used almost exclusively by "spiritual" gurus, appears to be moving into the public domain and common usage, thus increasing the frequency of my annoyance.

As might be expected, I began to wonder at my obvious irritation. At first I thought it might be a consequence of my long and eventually unpleasant association with a hierarchical (higherarchical?) church structure in which some people, by virtue of various ordinations, were considered to be more "filled with the Holy Spirit" than others and thus positioned higher on the spiritual ladder. However, this answer to my questioning self failed to satisfy.

With further reflection, I began to realize that the concept of a "higher self" is inconsistent with my experience and understanding of the universe as an open, dynamic "holosystem" rather than a power hierarchy – an interactive, interconnected creative process rather than a spiritual ladder for human improvement.

My active participation in this process depends not on my "highness" or degree of perfection, but rather on my realness, my willingness to be fully who I am, and on my trust in the ongoing process. To the extent that I am in touch with and giving expression to my own center or core or soul self, I am also in touch with and giving expression to the "informed consciousness" of the universe. Needless to say, this awareness will be tempered by my human limitations.

My bias on this issue is no doubt a consequence of the way in which I came into this broader consciousness. I was not trying to meditate myself into a higher consciousness when this shift occurred, in fact I had never heard of such a state and would never have thought to try to attain it. Rather, I was confronted with an overwhelming personal crisis which demanded new ways of seeing and functioning if I was to survive.

On the basis of inner knowing and the recalling of some words of wisdom from a childhood Sunday school teacher, I made the seemingly risky and very frightening choice to live and act as best I could according to certain values: self–acceptance and self–responsibility; personal honesty as inseparable from love; letting go of the need to control in favor of trusting the life process; self–direction based on inner awareness rather than outer conformity.

The immediate consequence of this choice was an incredible sense of relief and an awareness of my unique personhood, of my connection to all of life, and of my belonging to the universe. This new consciousness arose much more from being my real self than from any idea of a higher self, had more to do with a dynamic process (holomovement?) than a "higher" level of functioning and with becoming whole than with becoming perfect by doing things the "right" way.

In recent years I have become acutely aware of the need for a new vocabulary to represent new experiences and understandings, with terms such as holographic and holomovement as ways of describing and perceiving our life process and our participation in the creative life of the universe. There seems to be a further need for a word related to self which describes the person as an active participant and co–creator in the cosmic creative process. "Holoself" seems to be a good choice, emphasizing the wholeness of the person as an expression of and participant in the wholeness/holiness of life.

At the invitation of the editor of the AHP Perspective, Deborah Breed, I was invited to be the guest editor of the October 1988 issue. Following is my introduction to that issue.

Over the centuries we human beings have found ourselves in all kinds of difficulties because of our inability to distinguish among experience, belief and fact. We tend to confuse our inner experience with our explanation of that experience and then find ourselves in conflict with others as we defend (sometimes very belligerently!) the "truth" of our explanations.

Such confusion is apparent when Christians claim to know that Jesus died for their sins because they experience relief and new life when they "accept Jesus as Lord and Savior" .They fail to grasp that such a sense of renewal flows naturally from releasing guilt feelings and experiencing acceptance, no matter whether the belief that brings us to this new freedom is based on fact or fiction.

As with the effectiveness of a placebo, the real issue is what goes on "in here" in our perception rather than "out there" in the world of facts and fiction. It seems obvious that beliefs and belief systems are a necessary aspect of our human functioning. Serious problems arise, however, when we fail to distinguish between experience and belief, when we do not recognize that our beliefs are never infallible but always subject to continuing correction and expansion with new information if we are to grow in the wisdom that leads to personal and planetary peace.

Our forum authors address this issue from several perspectives and bring, we hope, greater clarity to a subject that should be clear, but so often is obscure.

Belief and the Open Mind

WHEN I WAS ELEVEN YEARS old, I began attending Sunday school classes at an Episcopal church at the invitation of some friends. Two years later, when all the other members of my class were to be confirmed, I of course wanted to be confirmed along with them. I wanted to belong, and the price of admission was a "profession of faith" as set forth in a creed. It never occurred to me to question the statements I was required to make; at eleven I had little basis for raising questions even if I had thought to do so. In any case, my need to belong was greater than my need to know, and it wasn't until almost twenty years later that my need to know surpassed my need to belong.

Recently a young friend of mine was caught in a more dramatic choice between believing or not belonging. At a time when she was feeling especially lonely and vulnerable after ending a long–term relationship, a group of charis- matic Christians took her into their midst and gave her warmth and security. Soon, however, her new friends told her that if she wanted to continue as a member of their group, she would have to ask her Jewish roommate to move out. In her state of emotional need she agonized over the decision, but came to realize that she couldn't possibly ask the best roommate she had ever had to move out simply because she wasn't a Christian.

Needless to say, most conflicts between believing and belonging are not nearly this blatant and dramatic. Usually they are more subtle, more difficult to perceive and therefore to resolve.

Many of us grow up with little or no awareness of how often and how much we adjust our perceiving to accommodate our needs for acceptance, approval and belonging. It often takes a life–size crisis to shake us up to the reality of the situation. For me it was just such a crisis, when the church to which I belonged was unable to meet my emotional and intellectual needs, that pressured me into a new awareness, a new way of seeing. At that point I had more to gain by breaking out than by staying in.

Soon afterwards, studying the prophet Isaiah for a course in the Old Tes- tament at theological seminary, I came to see that understanding is always a consequence of openness to new information and seeing new connections, that any claim to a "final revelation" is as ridiculous in religion as in any other area of human study. That spelled the end or my commitment to any doctrinaire position. Several years later, in the introduction to *On Becoming a Person*, I was delighted to find that Carl Rogers had had a similar experience while in seminary.

Fortunately more and more people seem to recognize that any fundamentalism blocks the creative learning process. A closed mind, whether capitalist or communist, Christian, Muslim, Buddhist or Hindu, Darwinian, creationist or humanist, is a destructive force in our midst, often forcing children to close their own minds in order to survive in a world of powerful adults who demand belief as a price of acceptance. Parents and teachers, often unknowingly, tend to use emotional blackmail to convince children that there is only one "right" way.

We of the humanistic and transpersonal persuasion like to think of ourselves as beyond such tactics, but at times we, too, confuse "belief about" with "experience of", confuse explanations of our mental images with the images themselves, confuse the map with the terrain. We forget that while actual experience is undeniable, beliefs about and explanations of that experience are always subject to correction with further experience.

Beliefs can be valuable maps as we find our way through life, as long as we think of them as part of the learning process rather than ultimate truth.

Chapter 6

A HUMAN THEOLOGY

New Understandings of God as Creative Spirit

There are addictions to drugs, to lifestyles, to the affection of another person, to knowledge, to having more and more weapons, or to a higher and higher gross national product. There are addictions to outmoded dogmas, for which people are still massacring each other the world over.

Stephen Nachmanovitch,
FREE PLAY:
The Power of Improvisation in Life and the Arts

Religion, like modern science, thrives on reductionism. Although it claims to open us up to the mystery of God and to the mystery of life, it attempts to do so through a series of religious and legal requirements which stymie our spiritual creativity. Religion leaves us with an anthropocentric image of God, and seriously fractures the essential oneness of reality. We are left with a fragmented sense of who we are and what our role in the world is all about.

Diarmuid O'Murchu,
RELIGION IN EXILE:
A Spiritual Homecoming

Love is a dynamic relationship, a two–way exchange of energy. When God is conceived as an omniscient and omnipotent Prime Mover, no such energy is generated. Entropy ensues, the universe becomes a cold and empty place, and the Great Work will never be done.

Parker J. Palmer,
AN ACTIVE LIFE:
Wisdom for Work, Creativity, and Caring

$\mathcal{D}$own through the centuries, religious, cultural and political purists of every ilk have more often than not been at war with each other as well as committing horrendous crimes against those who stray from narrow doctrinal paths. We decry such outrageous acts as the Crusades, the Inquisition, the burning of witches, the Holocaust, and ethnic cleansing, and yet the terrible hostility of the so–called faithful against infidels continues in our midst. Millions cling to archaic definitions of Divinity, often ready to take up arms and bombs in defense of those definitions.

Our local newspaper (as of 2005) occasionally carries an inserted section paid for by a group of " Christian" churches. A recent editorial stated that in matters of belief, church members must be narrow–minded. This of course is not new information, but I have never before seen it stated so blatantly by a member of a Christian church. What those holding to this view fail to realize is that much of the violence in today's world is a direct consequence of such narrow–mindedness, especially since they tend to insist that others hold the same view.

This editorial brought to mind a paper I wrote many years ago in response to an item in the religion section of TIME magazine. The ideas I expressed in the paper are at least as relevant today as they were in the nineteen–seventies regarding religion/spirituality issues, if not the status of the theological seminaries. Since the paper continues to be timely, I include it here as food for thought even for those who claim little interest in theology.

Theology in a New Key

AN ITEM IN THE RELIGION section of TIME magazine (March 8, 1976) concerning the "Fading Big Five" (Union Theological Seminary and the divinity schools at Harvard, Yale, Chicago and Vanderbilt Universities) raised the question of their place and purpose in relationship to American Protestant church life and thought. Should they try to regain their standing with their "once primary clients", the Protestant churches who formerly hired the great majority of their graduates with basic divinity degrees but now hired less than half, or is their another alternative?

A report from the Rockefeller Foundation, authored by theologian George Lindbeck and social scientists Karl Deutsch and Nathan Glazer, decried the increasing lack of community, the decline in scholarly rigor, and the decreasing commitment to specific religious traditions which appeared to have brought the schools to their present state of waning influence on American Protestantism. In outlining a remedy for the situation, the report called for a return to "particularism" in commitment to specific religious orientations and for a greater "pluralism" of representation of religious groups such as conservative evangelicals.

I find these suggestions very depressing in that they seem to serve only one purpose, the reinforcement of the established churches. They lack apparent regard for whether the religious establishment or the usually static theology of particularism are in fact effectively meeting the spiritual needs of American society in general or of the Big Five theology students in particular.

A number of years ago I attended the monthly meetings of a local chapter of the Academy of Religion and Mental Health. Most of the participants were either practicing psychiatrists, parish clergy, or seminary professors. While discussions were often interesting, I soon came to realize that we were unlikely to become truly creative in our exchanges. Because most of the discussants were deeply committed to and found their security in certain basic assumptions about the nature of human beings which they were not about to question, creative integration was not possible. They were interested in finding how their beliefs and concerns overlapped, but not in questioning or letting go of their existing theological and psychological concepts in favor of a search for a more adequate body of theory concerning the nature of man.

The same situation seemed to exist in theological schools. There was often an attempt to incorporate psychological theory into a theological framework, without apparent concern for contradictions between the two systems and without thought of moving to a new level of integration. Of course there are exceptions Carl Rogers, while a student at Union Theological Seminary (1924–1926), was fortunate enough to have contact with Dr. A. C. McGiffert and a few others who were committed to the process of free inquiry at any cost.

Rogers and some of his fellow students formed a seminar group to consider questions which were bothering them, with the result that many of them thought themselves out of the ministry as a profession. A major block to continuing was the idea of having to make a commitment to specific unchanging beliefs in order to remain within a church's doctrinal limits.

S. T. Hayakawa has spoken of three stages of organization, around a physical symbol, verbal symbols, and shared perceptions. It would seem that many of the difficulties we are presently experiencing in our society and especially in the area of religion stem from the fact that our increasing awareness of broader possibilities makes organization on older concepts (i. e., place of worship or stated belief system) impossible. The problem is that making the transition from one stage to the next is very difficult, and our present challenge to move into stage three is no exception. We are having to learn to trust our own perceptions, find the freedom to share them with others, and amend them as required by new experiences in order to conceive of new kinds of organic communities which incorporate the seeming paradox of individual autonomy and group cohesion.

Not only the theological schools but many of our other institutions are in the throes of just such a struggle. Since the people involved in those institutions are functioning at different levels of awareness, no one model of organization can satisfy everyone. In the area of education, alternative schools or alternative tracks within the same school may be the best we can do at the present time. An institution such as Union Theological Seminary might offer three options: 1. "church life" for those who are comfortable with their belief systems and wish to train for traditional parish ministry; 2. "creative theology" for those committed to an open–ended and scholarly search for new understanding and expression of the nature of God; and 3. "personal studies" for those who want to explore their own inner world, find their own direction and clarify their personal beliefs.

Beyond such an arrangement, perhaps the so–called liberal theological schools should abandon altogether the task of indoctrinating persons for a parish ministry. They might leave that to denominational training schools, and focus instead on an inter–disciplinary approach to exploring humanity's spiritual nature without any of the restrictions of a commitment to earlier doctrines or a division of disciplines. The time is long past when the nature of life can be divided into neat pockets of theology, psychology, biology, physics, etc.

The "Big Five' and other similar schools of theology could serve a dynamic purpose on the educational scene by serving as centers of communication for those who choose to explore the frontiers of an emerging faith in the energy/consciousness which is Life. They could adopt as their theme "commitment to new ways of seeing, communion in new ways of being".

Recent and current campaigns by religious Fundamentalists to impose on their fellow citizens the beliefs in which they have been indoctrinated is not only dismaying but frightening. Even more dismaying is that many who do not themselves hold to such beliefs seem to accept the claim on the part of the President of the United States in 2005 that he talks to God. There seems to be no recognition that he speaks to a concept of god in which he has been indoctrinated by Fundamentalist Christians, a concept which bears little resemblance to emerging views of the Divine. To assume that a literal approach to religion and religious doctrines is somehow more moral than alternative liberal or even secular views of spirituality poses a dangerous threat to a democratic society. It was with these issues in mind that I wrote the following paper.

Christianity: An Alternative View

Openness to New Possibilities

ALONG WITH MILLIONS OF OTHER children, I was indoctrinated at an early age with the image of a God who required the death of his "only begotten Son" on a cross in order for me (along with millions of others) to be forgiven my sins. This was not the message in my younger years, however, when I was taught that Jesus loved me according to our song, "Jesus loves me this, I know, for the Bible tells me so: Little ones to him belong, we are weak and He is strong". This was a comforting thought, even though I had trouble making a real connection with this Jesus of my imagination.

I am reminded of the story about the little boy who kept getting out of bed and asking for a drink of water, then "another story", etc., but was repeatedly sent back to bed by his mother. Finally he said, "But Mommy, I'm lonely," to which she replied that he should go back to bed and remember that Jesus loved him. There was a moment of silence before the boy replied, "But Mommy, I want love with skin on it!"

As I progressed through classes of Sunday school, the message of the Crucifixion became more obvious, along with the love story. It never occurred to me to question why a loving father god would be so "mean" as to send his son to die on a cross for the sins of the world. It took a spiritual identity crisis of meaning and purpose when I was thirty–one years old to bring about a subsequent re–thinking of the Christian doctrinal message, and with it the loss of my religious communities. It is unfortunate that being true to one's own understanding often means the loss of community, and yet fortunate that it can lead to a more diverse and accepting community.

Eventually I came to understand that the level of human consciousness at the time of Jesus, at least in his part of the world, was such that inner conflicts were projected onto outer gods, devils and demons. Attempts to meet inner needs for love, security, and self–worthiness were sought in outer solutions, hence such concepts as the Jewish scapegoat ritual to deal with sins. The subsequent Christian teaching that Jesus' death on the cross bought us forgiveness of sins meant relief from feelings of guilt. With this new freedom came a sense of being "born again" or seeing the world with new eyes, as though for the first time. In line with what we now know about the placebo effect, it was the *belief* in forgiveness that brought the sense of relief, not the death on the cross. Many have experienced the same sense of new birth without believing in redemption by Jesus' death on the cross.

What I came to believe about the Crucifixion was that powerful men, both religious and secular and with a power limited to their positions in society, were seriously threatened by the personal power of Jesus, the power of truth and compassion which spoke to the human soul. Thus it was that Jesus had to go, and he went in the way that was common at the time for criminals and political foes of the Roman Empire.

It may be that Jesus expected his Father God to save him from the painful ending, a Father to replace Joseph, who apparently disappeared from his life in early adolescence. But Jesus then turned the situation around when he said, "Father, forgive them, for they know not what they do" That, for me, is the meaning of redemption: the transformation of a very destructive situation into one of creative good. The story of Joseph in the Old Testament teaches much the same lesson: having been sold down the river by his brothers, Joseph transformed a bad situation into a good outcome.

What Christianity has seemingly failed to acknowledge is the shift in consciousness to an inner awareness and greater understanding of the workings of the human psyche. We now can look to childhood mistreatment, trauma and abandonment rather than "original sin" as causes of later tragedies, including homicide and suicide. We can understand lack of self-worth and depression as loss of respect for the unique human soul, as our personhood is defined by the culture into which we are born or by our rebellion against that culture.

This is not a problem in the world of nature, in that an acorn has no choice but to become an oak tree if it becomes anything at all. For an acorn to become a maple tree is not an option. We humans, on the other hand, do indeed try to become other than who we are. Our growing consciousness over the centuries and our long childhood dependency on others have left us vulnerable to the demands of others in determining the persons we become, often resulting in serious conflict and confusion. Lynn Stoddard, in his remarkable little book, *Educating for Human Greatness*, brings this issue into focus with his three "I"s, Identity, Interaction, and Inquiry, although not from a theological perspective.

It would appear that the time has come when only an upgrading of our understanding of who we are as human beings and of our relationship to each other, our planet and the cosmos can save us from the terrible destruction of human life and nature that now challenges us. The claims of religious Fundamentalists that their particular definitions of God are the only true interpretations have brought us to the brink of disaster. Especially heinous are those who claim that their god commands them to murder innocent people in his name. Such a misunderstanding of the Creative Spirit of the Cosmos could bring about our demise as the human race.

Perhaps no one says it better than Brian Swimme : "Our primary teacher is the universe. The universe evokes our being, supplies us with creative energy, insists on a reverent attitude toward everything, and liberates us from our puny self–definition." Are we willing to commit ourselves to a creative and unifying way of being, thinking, feeling, and acting in order to save ourselves and our planet?

Chapter 7

RELATIONSHIPS AND COMMUNITY

Questions of Trust and Mistrust

The key building block for sustainable relationships is trust. Trust is a bond that evolves as two persons get to know each other and experience safety in opening their hearts to each other. Trust develops when you respect one another's needs and develop a history of common experience and caring.

Linda Marks,
LIVING WITH VISION
Reclaiming the Power of the Heart

Trust creates the flow and gentles the mindbodyspirit. When I trust myself I am able to enter fully into the process of discovering and creating who I am. When I trust my own inner processes I am able to become what I am meant to become. When I trust you I am able to allow you in. And when I trust the processes of living I am able to join others in the life journey.

Trust enriches my spirit; fear robs it.

Trust and fear are keys to understanding persons and social systems. When trust is high, relative to fear, people and social systems function well..

Trust is an integrating and wholizing force.

Trust provides an environment that nourishes personal growth, holistic health, spirituality, and the discovery of the soul.

Jack R. Gibb,
TRUST:
A new view of PERSONAL and
ORGANIZATIONAL development

Over the past few years, several close and long–time friends have died of cancer. In each case the person suffering the sickness refused to give expression to inner feelings, either past or present, through journal writing, art therapy, or any form of counseling therapy. I wrote the following piece in response to my questions and concerns about the wisdom of being honest with ourselves and trusting our own process. It has been edited to clarify some points and to protect personal identities.

Love And Truth

MANY YEARS AGO WHILE STILL in my Christian churchgoing and Bible–reading mode, I read in one of the Epistles that we should not do "in the dark" anything that we would not do "in the light". Eventually I came to understand that openness about the persons we are is not only a Christian guideline, but a basic principle of creative living. Deceiving ourselves and/or others is not only harmful to relationships, but costs us energy and is against our natural inclination to be "real". An inner conflict between the need to be our soul–centered selves and yet live up to the expectations of others can prove to be life–denying.

My painful experience over the past few years has been the loss of several persons from my life who were all very loving, caring human beings and yet had been dishonest with themselves or others or both. While I cannot say what went on in their minds and hearts, I do know that they were very dependent on the love, respect, and even admiration of others for their own sense of worth.

At least for some of them, denial of their own "shadow", including pains of the past and fears for the future, was their chosen path. They preferred the choice of "positive" feelings and beliefs under all circumstances, not acknowledging the existence of "negative" feelings underlying their conscious attitudes. Some who were suffering what proved to be terminal cancer were relying on the positive prayers of hundreds of concerned friends and prayer groups to bring them back to health.

Two examples of the denial of the inner shadow were two women, both my close friends for many years and both of whom had taken up painting in their later years. One was serious enough about her art that she had exhibited and sold several of her pieces. When these two women became ill with cancer, both were encouraged to use their painting to express their inner feelings, and both refused to do so. One was encouraged to participate in an art therapy group for cancer patients, went to it once, felt that she would vomit, and never went back. The other was encouraged by a friend skilled in journal writing to express her feelings in writing as well as art, but would not consider it.

Several friends and acquaintances who have recently died of cancer had been involved in extra–marital affairs at various times in their lives. Such activity involved dishonesty with their own spouses or their lovers' spouses or both. The problem as I see it is not the affair per se, but the lack of respect for the betrayed partners. The lovers often excused their secrecy by saying that they didn't want to hurt their spouses, or that their spouses didn't want to know or didn't care anyway. In contrast to this approach is that of a couple known to me who have a so–called "open marriage" contract, which frees them to have affairs with others without the dishonesty problem, at least in relationship to each other.

What I am questioning is whether we can be truly loving without being honest in relationships with both self and others; whether any degree of personal integrity is possible without awareness, acceptance, acknowledgement and expression of who we are (at least to the best of our ability at each stage of life); and whether the fragmentation which accompanies secrecy may compromise our immune system.

My interest in this matter is of course personal. Many years ago, at a time of personal crisis, I faced these issues myself. It was a commitment to being honest that saved me from an extra–marital disaster and brought me to the point where my own integrity was more important to me than the opinion of others. While this was my own choice, I do not judge others for the choices they make. I do question, however, whether I would be able to trust them in a relationship with me when they are dishonest with others. I also wonder whether I should be more outspoken on the issue in light of my experience.

The reason I wonder about this is because in a small group meeting in which one member was sharing with the group about extra–marital relationships of which her husband was ignorant, I never "spoke my own truth", I suppose because I was never asked. Part of the problem for me is in having information about a situation in which, from my perspective, the persons who have the greatest right to that information are kept in the dark. I feel as though I am a party to the deception. This might never have been an issue had we adopted ground rules like those for a "circle of trust" as described by Parker J. Palmer in his book, A HIDDEN WHOLENESS, providing a setting of safety from violation and for a commitment to speak one's own truth.

Many years ago I found myself in a similar predicament when a young girl pregnant out of wedlock (interesting word) came to live with our close neighbors and friends. She gave her baby for adoption to the neighbor couple who already had six children and considered themselves ideal parents, while keeping the child's whereabouts secret from the birth father and his parents who wanted to raise the child. I felt uncomfortable being a party to such knowledge about the situation, but saw no solution to my discomfort, so I lived with it.

So – where do I draw the line? I can't very well divest myself of unwanted information once I have it, nor do I feel free to bring it out in the open when it involves the lives of others. How can I receive unwanted information without being dishonest myself, or at least feeling fragmented? How can I trust someone in friendship when I know that person to be secretive or dishonest with others? In the words of the King of Siam in "The King and I", it's a puzzlement.

While I ponder these matters, I continue to question and explore the relationship, if any, between love, honesty, and the health of the immune system.

In our present society, we are being bombarded with news of dishonesty in high places, especially in some of the largest corporations in North America. We are also being confronted with the unfortunate consequences of secrecy and manipulation on the part of top management, creating an atmosphere of mistrust in organizations large and small. Just recently, in an article in the San Jose Mercury News (November 13, 2005), the departure of Carly Fiorina as CEO of Hewlett–Packard is blamed on her arrogant management style in direct opposition to the "HP Way". The latter is described as "an ethos of restraint, responsibility and trust" resulting in a sense of competency and wholeness which in the past has served the company well.

My own experience has been entirely with non–profit organizations, first in church settings and later with human service organizations and educational institutions. Many of those experiences have been positive and some negative. The minister of a church to which I once belonged, when asked why he went into the ministry responded that it was for the power! That explained why he was secretive and manipulative in his relationship to the congregation. Most people in management are not so naively open about their motivation.

My good experiences, whether as a board member, an executive director or program coordinator, an educator or support staff, have always been in situations in which the relationships between the various stakeholders have been open and trusting, even in times of conflict of opinions.

I thought I was in such a positive environment when offering a program in a community college, only to find out that I was mistaken. I recently came across an old memo in which I was reminded of a very bad situation related to that program regarding a grant application I had submitted for scholarship funds for low–income persons wanting to take the course. I was wondering why the funds had not come through when I ran into the Ministry representative responsible for the grant, and when I asked him why we had not received the money, he informed me that it had been forwarded to the college several weeks previously.

A college administrator had simply taken the money and used it for other purposes without ever letting me know that it had come through.

A friend who is principal of a charter school serving very low–income families has recently had a similar experience, with the school district having absorbed thousands of dollars of her grant money for its own purposes without her knowledge or permission. An earlier change in administration had resulted in considerable mistrust in the district.

One of the worst examples of mistrust occurred in a community organization which I had left when the grant money for my position ran out. A competent member of our staff continued as project manager, but the new board president convinced the board members that the position required a person with an advanced degree. A new job description was written up and the existing manager was told she could apply, but of course she could not meet the new requirement. The president then informed the Unemployment Insurance people that the employee had left voluntarily and so could not qualify for insurance. Fortunately one of the organization board members informed the U. I. representative that the information was untrue, so the ex–manager received unemployment insurance. The organization, by the way, failed to survive more than a few months following this event.

While the great majority of my organizational experiences have been very positive, one which occurred many years ago proved to be a nightmare. I describe it in a severely edited form (to protect personal and organizational identity) as follows.

Organization X At The Crossroads

ON THE BASIS OF MY past year's experience and especially my six months as a contract staff member of Organization X, I have come to the conclusion that Esalen's law as articulated by Richard Price ("You always teach others what you most need to learn yourself.") applies equally well to this organization. While we are eager to put on large conferences for the purpose of popularizing our principles and for making money to support the spread of those principles, we seem less than eager to practice same in our organizational life together.

Perhaps it is simply a matter of ignorance on our part, or perhaps those persons most responsible for the current processes and direction of the organization consider the issue unimportant for its effective functioning. Whatever the reason, my hope is to present a reasonably clear picture of our present situation as I see it so that we can discuss the issues and make well–informed choices consistent with our principles as to our future direction. I would also hope that in presenting and participating in a major educational conference on leadership, we will *not* prove to be our own worst students.

My concern about these issues is personal as well as organizational. During fifteen years as a community volunteer in a wide variety of associations, and during another fifteen years as a professional educator and administrator, I have almost always been given full responsibility for "whole jobs". I can think of only two exceptions, both situations in which I was working for insecure administrators who were afraid that their jobs or reputations would be jeopardized unless I did things their way. Unfortunately, they seldom knew more and often knew less about the issues than I did, and the experience left me feeling frustrated and discouraged – and also a bit (!) annoyed.

A story by Robert Townsend in his book FURTHER UP THE ORGANIZATION seems to apply. He tells of a small publisher responsible for a daily newsletter that had to be at the printer by 7 p.m. but seldom made the deadline. The six editors responsible for the content were second–guessed over and over by the president and managing editor. The owner of the company decided to fire the president, managing editor and secretary, and create a partnership of the six editors. After a time for adjustment, the new arrangement worked wonderfully well, with the copy going to the printer by late afternoon.

I am not suggesting that the top management of Organization X or any other organization in a similar situation be fired, but ideally that they become partners rather than supervisors, with specific areas of responsibility in terms of job definition within the partnership structure. Admittedly the effectiveness of such a structure depends on the ability of each staff person to work independently in his/her area of expertise and the willingness to be responsible to the team in terms of personal performance and open communication.

In Robert Townsend's example, the owner was in a position to know his editors well enough to take the risk required to try out the new structure. He knew they were competent in their own areas of responsibility, but he could not know in advance whether they would work together effectively as a partnership. It took an act of faith on his part, plus perhaps some desperation about the existing miserable situation, to be willing to experiment with a whole new process. A similar combination of knowledge and willingness to risk would be required of the board of directors, management and staff of Organization X.

At issue here is the value of self–control and self–direction as opposed to other–control and other–direction as utilized in the typical heirarchical, supervisor–supervisee relationship. The idea that such other–control is even possible in the information age is subject to question. A broader base of human awareness and a more open system of information exchange legislates against the ultimate effectiveness of such control, as Nixon discovered in the Watergate fiasco.

In the work situation as in politics, more and more people are insisting on empowering themselves in the decision–making process rather than leaving it to others who may be no wiser – or even less wise – than they themselves. What is needed is a "learning environment" rather than an experts–know–it–all or managers–have–the–answers attitude.

The question is whether this organization can become the kind of learning community in which staff, board directors, and members can participate in the learning, problem–solving, planning and decision–making processes which directly affect their particular work, responsibilities, or services, or whether the leaders who happen to be in office at the time will make decisions affecting everyone based on their own "expert" answers. The latter approach seems especially unsuitable for an organization in which the board leadership changes every year, and therefore the expert answers along with it.

Both the stability and flexibility of an on–going open learning community seems like a more appropriate base for planning and decision–making, In such a community, as Don Michael ("Neither Hierarchy nor Anarchy", from RETHINKING LIBERALISM, Walter Truett Anderson, Ed.) states it, "The locus of authority varies with the task, in which autonomy is dependent on the effective operation of the whole system, and vice versa."

The importance of interpersonal openness became apparent recently in relationship to the management of an annual meeting. For many years the major portion of the work involved in mounting such a meeting has been contributed by the office staff including a meeting coordinator, with varying measures of success depending on the relationship between the office staff, the program committee, and the site committee if there was one.

In the case of the most recent meeting, the program committee decided (according to their own report) that the office staff were incapable of putting on a successful meeting, even though they knew nothing about the skills and experience of the recently hired coordinator. They decided that they themselves would take over as much control of the conference as they could. Unfortunately they failed to communicate this information to the staff as those who would be most seriously affected by their decision, and so the new meeting coordinator was hired to fill a position which subsequently proved not to exist. By the time the truth came out several months later, on direct confrontation of the program committee by a staff member, the damage had been done.

If the members of the committee had been open with the staff at the outset of the planning process as to their misgivings and intentions, clear decisions could have been made at that time as to who would be responsible for what. This would have prevented many of the subsequent misunderstandings, logistical mix–ups, and considerable unnecessary expense. I need to add that my own failure to insist on a clear job description as meeting coordinator and a contract outlining responsibilities, an honest statement of expectations on both sides, obviously contributed to the problem. Since no written job description was available, I depended on information given to me by staff and by a previous (and successful) meeting coordinator who had no way of knowing that the new set–up would be so different. With such a clearly stated agreement from which to work, the changes in locus of responsibilities could have been mutually determined in advance, or at least would have become more obvious as they occurred.

It seems to me that the organization is at such a point in its own history and development that this kind of action is called for, and that in our closeness to our own organization, we are in danger of not seeing the woods for the trees. I also believe that the kind of original, unprecedented action which author Bill Torbert describes can only emerge from an open, self–managed learning community. Such a community existed at a recent organizational retreat when some positive steps were taken to facilitate intra–organizational relationships.

Unfortunately, once the immediate administrative emergency was met, it seemed that the restructuring work was no longer seen as relevant to the welfare of the organization. The members of the committee appointed to research and report on restructuring issues were not invited to participate, or even to sit in as observers, on a recent executive committee meeting concerned with staff restructuring decisions. This action appears to disenfranchise the restructuring committee even as a facilitating body for open discussion on structural changes. If this is indeed the case, it needs to be stated openly and clearly so that everyone involved understands the situation and does not hold false expectations as to the degree of participation planned by the executive.

In concluding my comments, it is my sincere hope that the organization will make a clear–cut decision and statement as to its intended direction, whatever that decision may be. Only on that basis can those of us with a long–time commitment to Organization X make a realistic decision as to the extent of our future commitment.

As a long–time and well–informed member of the organization pointed out to me on reading my report, I made the mistake of assuming that the administration would adhere to its stated principles. Had I been employed by an organization which had no such stated high ideals, I would have had no such expectations and so not have been subject to such disillusionment. While I have continued my membership in the organization in the intervening years and seen great improvement in its operating principles, my involvement has been very limited.

I was subsequently fortunate in finding employment (at age sixty–four) in a situation where I was able to establish very much of a partnership relationship among the staff and volunteers with a strong emphasis on individual responsibility, cooperation, and clear communication. Most of the time this approach worked very well (there were a few blips along the way!), including the relationship with an advisory board of members from the larger community who were well informed concerning the nature of our outreach and educational work with seniors. My last place of full time employment, with mandatory retirement at age seventy, has provided lasting friendships and occasional volunteer work, as well as the opportunity to create two booklets related to spirituality, aging, and well–being.

Chapter 8

PRISONS OF THE SOUL

Violation, Violence and Justice

Today we look at violence and we attempt to address sexual violence, racism, crime, gang violence, etc., as different entities, but there is only violence and all of these are expressions of it. In fact, our response to violence is itself violent, showing how deeply we miss this connection. I put it in terms of "deathful" action / "lifeful" action Deathful action increases the presence of deathful action . . . lifeful action increases the presence of "lifefulness". This is what Ghandi spoke of when he said the end is always determined by the means. A violent means will bring about a violent end, no matter how well intentioned.

A concept that's been very helpful to me is the separation of force and violence. Force is designed to oppose persons' destructive behavior, to stop them from doing it. Violence is designed to harm them. Yet force sometimes causes harm, but only as much as a person keeps insisting on hurting others. Violence uses force as well, but its intent is to cause harm, not to stop destructive behavior.

Troy Chapman,
excerpts from personal letters

*A*s we listen to the evening news, it is seldom that we hear stories of caring and outreach to those in distress except in cases of natural or accidental disasters. Most stories relate to some form of social violation or physical violence, from character assassination to physical assault and murder. Prisons, crowded beyond intended limits, are often called correctional institutions, although usually more given to punishing than correcting. Penitentiary is indeed a more appropriate name, since opportunities are seldom offered for personal transformations and new beginnings. What's more, we continue to assume that criminals are "bad apples" rather than "damaged goods" and that as long as they understand the difference between good and bad behavior, they are of course "sane" and therefore fit for trial. There appears to be no understanding in the criminal "justice" system, nor in the public at large, that there is such a thing as emotional intelligence which is a far better indicator of sanity – or lack of it – than head knowing.

My personal experience with the courts and penal systems is very limited. I have served on juries several times and considered the processes most inadequate for the problems presented, especially one dealing with a teen–age girl who was suing her former step–father for sexual abuse. The young girl appeared to have learning problems, and also may have been pushed into suing by her mother, angry that her former husband had left her for another woman. In my opinion, the courtroom was not the place for resolving such a problem, and may only have made matters worse for the girl, since her former step–father was declared not guilty.

My experience with prisons is also limited. I have only been inside the gates of a high–security correctional facility twice, both times to meet with prisoners about to be released into the community. The first session went very well, with considerable discussion about the problems and possible solutions of moving out into the community. The second session, however, was something of a disaster, with one prisoner disrupting any possible discussion by loudly claiming many times over that he couldn't wait to get out and get even with the guy who put him there. Unfortunately I did not know how to defuse the situation.

Despite my very limited hands–on experience related to these issues, I have never–theless had an intense interest in the causes of violation and violence for many years. While attending college, I lost very dear friends to the hostilities of WWII, which appeared to be the epitome of violence. Then came news of the unthinkable atrocities of the Holocaust. A number of years later, while watching the film The Bridge on the River Kwai, I determined to search for causes of violence not only in society, but in the personal lives of human beings. The theme of this book, while seemingly unrelated to such a quest, is in fact the story of such a search.

Some years ago an educator specializing in so–called learning disabilities estimated that as high as sixty percent of imprisoned criminals suffered from such limitations. Because of a deep personal interest and concern about this issue, I wrote the following concerning two separate legal cases which appeared to have some circumstances in common. Since the introduction to each piece was the same, I have combined them into one article.

Consulting The Wrong Experts?

As LONG AGO AS 1959 a book appeared on the market entitled INDIVIDU-AL BEHAVIOR: A PERSONAL APPROACH TO BEHAVIOR. The authors, A. W. Combs and D. Snygg, explain how our behavior relates to the way we see and understand or fail to understand ourselves and the world in which we live. In a more recent textbook on HELPING RELATIONSHIPS by Combs, Avila, and Purkey, the authors describe Perceptual Psychology as taking the position that "each of us does at every moment what seems appropriate at that moment" according to how we perceive and comprehend ourselves and our world. Further, they say that "when the nature of perception is understood, even the *weirdest behavior* becomes comprehensible". They point out that while this fact may seem very obvious, our failure to recognize and act on it may be the single most important cause of human misunderstanding, conflict, misery and maladjustment.

This information calls to mind a developmental problem well known to educational psychologists and neurologists as a "perceptual handicap", a form of learning disability which can severely distort the ways in which children suffering from such a handicap perceive and understand their worlds. These misperceptions often lead to seemingly odd behaviors, which in turn lead to their rejection by other people.

One way in which children with such perceptual distortion deal with their experiences of rejection and failure is to develop their own imaginary worlds in which they can succeed on their own terms without regard for reality. Unless the adults in their lives tune in to their inner worlds and help them develop a healthy sense of reality, they may be on their way to tragic consequences in adulthood.

The problem is especially apparent for a boy growing up in a wealthy family of achievers. Accustomed to a high standard of living and surrounded by other family members who are making it financially in a big way, he experiences himself as a total failure. He often loses all sense of personal identity unless someone recognizes his predicament and helps him to find his way out of it.

The issue is further complicated by the fact that wealthy parents often bail their children out of situations instead of helping them to deal with consequences in a realistic way. This is especially harmful to children with perceptual handicaps in that their sense of reality is distorted even further, allowing them to live in a world of no consequences for their behavior.

(Note: the "Chowchilla Kidnappers" were three young men who hijacked a busload of twenty-six school children and their driver in the summer of 1976, driving them to a gravel quarry and burying them in a van in hopes of getting a ransom.)

In light of the foregoing information, I would like to ask whether those charged with defending and judging Frederick Woods and James and Richard Schoenfeld have made any serious attempt to enter into their world and to understand their admittedly "weird behavior" from their point of view? Why did it apparently make sense to them, but not to the rest of the world?

The public defender has been quoted as saying that the kidnapping was undertaken by "three not too brilliant men". Has any action been taken to determine whether the three may in fact suffer from "minimal brain damage" and/or "neurological handicaps", forms of disability which were largely unrecognized at the time they were in school and which could have a serious effect on their ability to relate successfully to their world? Such learning disabilities, while not as obvious as other kinds of handicaps, can cause lasting emotional damage if not diagnosed and remedied. Such damage is not readily discernible in a standard psychiatric examination, at least not in terms of the current definition of legally sane/insane.

Beyond the possible problem of perceptual handicaps, has anyone discussed with qualified psychologists how badly young persons' sense of reality can be distorted if they have wealthy parents who persist in bailing them out of all their difficulties instead of helping them to understand that they live in a world of consequences?

Fred Woods' extensive collection of cars in various stages of disrepair is a case in point. No young man of lesser means could possibly have collected so many cars without having to take responsibility for disposing them in some way. And what kind of consequence was a fine of $125 for young men of such wealth when they went joyriding in 1974? How many young men who are unable to succeed in school and hold down good jobs have easy access to guns, panel trucks, trailer trucks and gravel pits, no questions asked? Surely this kind of wealth with no accountability leads to a gross distortion of reality even for young people of normal ability. When combined with a limited or handicapped intelligence, it can be disastrous.

I am in no way suggesting that Fred Woods and Rick and Jim Schoenfeld should not take responsibility and experience consequences for their activities on July 15, 1976. But I question whether life in prison is an appropriate consequence for three young men who may have had very little opportunity to learn the meaning of consequences and whose awareness of the seriousness of what they were doing may have been limited or even non–existent. It would be a most unusual prison situation which could provide the kind of learning environment that could compensate for the seeming deficiencies in their life education up to this point in time – a learning environment that could introduce them to the world of feeling, self–worth, and practical consequences.

(Note: John W. Hinckley, Jr., was found innocent by reason of insanity in 1982 for the shooting and wounding of President Ronald Reagan, Press Secretary James Brady and two others, and was committed to a mental hospital. He was thought to have acted out a movie script.)

John Hinckley is a prime example of a young man caught in a web of perceptual distortion, rejection and failure. With no anchor in personal identity and no moorings in healthy interpersonal relationships, he drifted or was tossed about in a world without bearings or direction – a likely candidate for entering the world of a movie script as though it were his own.

What has all this to do with sanity or insanity? What "experts" are in a position to determine who is sane? The dictionary (not psychiatric) meaning of sane is "healthy". Can any human being be considered truly healthy who attempts or commits kidnapping, assault, rape or murder against innocent persons? Is a person considered to be technically sane simply on the basis of intellectual knowledge of the definitions of right and wrong, regardless of the evidence of emotionally destructive behavior? Surely we would have put an end to personal and social violence long ago if it were a simple matter of head knowledge of right versus wrong.

Even if we could come up with a satisfactory definition of sanity in terms of mental, emotional and spiritual health, we are left with the current practice of consulting psychiatric experts whose theoretical framework may not allow for the kinds of questions appropriate to a particular situation. Very few psychiatrists are well informed on the kinds of developmental problems which regularly confront educational psychologists and which have so much effect on subsequent adult behavior.

Even if we develop a much more comprehensive understanding of the causes of human violence (hopefully, a distinct possibility in the near future), what will we do with that knowledge in terms of both prevention and rehabilitation? We have our work cut out for us, and it demands our full energy and attention in these times of increasing violence.

Chapter 9

MEANING AND PURPOSE

Key Issues for Aliveness

Systems that acknowledge their interdependence with their environment are *open* systems. Systems that don't are *closed*. This is the difference between being alive and being a machine.

In normative (closed) systems, those with the broadest responsibility are forever trying to prevent the boat from rocking. In integrative (open) systems, they steer it skillfully through turbulent and uncharted waters. They are truly visionary, equally at home in spiritual and material states.. . . ."being normal" and finding meaning in life are mutually exclusive.

Cliff Havener,
MEANING:
The Secret of Being Alive

At the heart of living with vision is purpose. Purpose is what compels us to take a stand, to act with such conviction that we may surprise ourselves, and ultimately is what fulfills us. We live from purpose at times without even knowing it. Without purpose life is at best incomplete, at worst futile. Our sense of purpose is what connects us to ourselves and to all of life.

Vision and purpose don't come from our minds. They come from the silence within – from the depths of the soul. Purpose becomes a question that will not go away.

Linda Marks,
LIVING WITH VISION:
Reclaiming the Power of the Heart

An Ultimate Question: Why Are We Here?

As I pointed out in the Introduction, it was a terrible sense of a lack of meaning and purpose in my life that was largely responsible for the crisis of spirit at age thirty–one. Whatever had given meaning to my life up to that point in time had evaporated without a trace, along with any zest for living. It was at this point of desperation that I recalled the words of my seventh grade Sunday school teacher which were to set me on a new path and result in the greatest surprise of my life: MEANING. Following is an article I wrote several years ago about her gift to me.

Thank You, Mrs. Loomis

AS A SMALL CHILD I was enrolled in a Sunday school class at a Congregational Church. For a year or so, my parents attended services at the same church, but eventually they gave up that practice and made me the sole representative of our family to visit "God's house" on Sunday morning.

I rather enjoyed my weekly sessions at Sunday school, especially the singing of such songs as "Jesus loves me" (that was encouraging) and "Up on the housetop, click, click, click, down through the Chimney with good St. Nick". When I was nine years old, my family moved to a new home four or five miles from the church, and I was no longer delivered to the weekly classes. Perhaps any further religious education was considered not important, at least not enough to merit the added time and effort.

After two years without benefit of religion, family friends offered to take me to Sunday school at their Episcopal Church. My mother urged me to go, perhaps because she thought it might help me to get over being so self–willed. I was not the compliant daughter that she would have liked, although I really tried to be the obedient child she envisioned.

In any case, I was duly enrolled in the new Sunday school, and our friends' daughter received a small gold cross for bringing me into the fold. I quite enjoyed the new church school as it was called. It was quite different from my earlier experience, in that all the classes were in one big room separated only by curtain dividers. The noise was sometimes deafening.

What made the time there special for me was our teacher, Mrs. Loomis, who I suppose must have been in her fifties or sixties, quite old from my perspective. She seemed to really like being there with her seventh–graders, and I felt more comfortable being myself with her on Sunday mornings than anywhere else during the week. I wasn't all that keen on some of the things we were required to do in class, such as memorize the names of all the books of the Bible and learn when to bow our heads and kneel to pray, but being appreciated for being myself made it worthwhile.

The following year we had a teacher who was nothing like Mrs. Loomis , dedicated to rules and rituals and proper church behavior. One Sunday when our class met in the church instead of the parish hall, the teacher was very displeased with those of us who were not wearing hats to signify our reverence in "God's house". I was so self–conscious that I put my gloves on my head, at which point she grabbed my gloves and hit me across the face with them. I left in tears and never went back to the class, but escaped into a Confirmation class with the rector. The year after that, at age thirteen, I was installed as teacher of a small group of third–grade girls.

Many years later at age thirty–one, I became depressed, feeling that my life was going nowhere, my marriage was that in name only, and my children were stuck with a not–very–good mother. I felt exhausted with trying to please everyone and to keep up with many church and community commitments. I experienced being pulled in far too many different directions. The thought occurred to me that I would just like to be myself, without having to earn the approval of others to feel worthwhile.

It was then, in a frightening "night of the soul" experience, that something Mrs. Loomis had told us came back to me, and may have saved my life. She had told us that God loved us just the way we were, not the way we ought to be. Being of a logical mind, I decided that on that basis, I had better put all my eggs in God's basket. Turning myself over to God so I could be myself was a fearful prospect, since I had no idea what God would expect of me (more expectations?) or whether anyone else would like me.

As it turned out, this choice was the major turning point in my life, with greater consequences than other turning points. The relaxation which I experienced resulted in better health, improved relationships, the ability to say no and set limits, growing awareness of myself as having unique gifts to contribute to community – and meaning.

There have certainly been many times since 1957 when I have lost my sense of direction, but never my sense of being at home with myself as a participant in the creative process we call life. Thank you, Mrs. Loomis, for your love and your wisdom.

Several years ago I received notice of a conference in British Columbia with a focus on Meaning. At first I thought I would like to attend the conference and explored the possibility of taking part in it, but then remembered that I am not at my best in meetings which are highly academic in nature. Reading research papers to large groups is simply not my thing. With this in mind, I forwarded several copies of the following paper to the coordinator of the conference for anyone who might pick it up to read. I never heard any more about it.

Meaning With A Big "M"

MUCH HAS BEEN WRITTEN AND said about meaning in recent years, but often no distinction is made between meaning with a big "M" and meaning with a little "m". We human beings often find meaning with a small "m" in many aspects of our lives such as our work, our families, our friendships, our intellectual pursuits, our hobbies, etc. The problem with having only small "m" meanings is that none of them are loss–proof at any stage in life, and especially as we grow older.

When I was thirty–one (over forty–five years ago), I was having difficulty finding even "m" meanings and became very depressed at seeing no reason for living. I recognized at the time that I was exhausted from being pulled in many different directions, trying to meet the expectations of myself and others as to how I ought to live my life. Whatever "m" meanings I had experienced previously had now fallen by the wayside. I could find no meaning or purpose in my life.

When this condition reached crisis proportions, I experienced a remarkable breakthrough by letting go of trying to meet any expectations and by just letting myself be. The most amazing aspect of this experience was discovering Meaning. I could not possibly have told you what it was, but I *felt it.* I now knew without any question that my life had Meaning. Subsequently I came to describe this shift as moving from a "restrictive" or "performance" mode of living to a "creative" or "integrative" (Cliff Havener's term) mode of living.

The experience of Meaning is the natural consequence of becoming participants in the ongoing creative process of all that is, giving expression to our own souls and no longer trying to find our vitality within the restrictions of family, religious, educational, political and cultural norms. In connecting with and living from our own souls, we experience not only Meaning, but connection with all of creation, a sense of oneness that was formerly lacking. This kind of Meaning cannot be taken away from us, since it is our birthright and provides a base from which to explore our own particular purpose – or purposes – during our time as residents of planet Earth.

It seems that at no time in history has our connection with the Creative Spirit of the Universe been more critical. At no time has there been a more desperate need to let go of our religious, cultural, and political belief systems as ultimate definitions of our lives, committing rather to creative process as our way of life and our defining mode of relating to ourselves, others, nature and planet. None but the creative way can bring compassion to our hearts, openness to our minds, health to our bodies, and oneness to our diversity. The time to commit is now.

A year or two ago, a notice of a contest on the topic of "The Power of Purpose" was posted on the Internet. Papers were to be submitted by a certain date and limited in length, and since the topic was of special interest to me, I decided to write such a paper and submit it by e-mail as directed. According to a report on the website, more than 70,000 papers were received from all over the world, so I was not too surprised although a bit disappointed that mine was not one of the winners. Since I don't have to win a contest to include the paper here. I'm offering it for your thought and consideration.

Purpose: Powerful Or Powerless?

As a young child, my purpose was made clear to me by my mother, which was above all else to be obedient. For my bedtime prayer, I was taught to say "God bless mommy and daddy and little brother, and make Rosalie a good girl". In my later years, I heard my mother say that obedience was the greatest virtue in a child. My father, on the other hand, did not seem to be a party to this grand purpose set forth for my early life.

In retrospect, it is no wonder that my mother and I were on a collision course. For many years I tried, I really tried, to do and be what my mother wanted because I so much wished for her approval. The problem is, of course, that our two greatest needs are to be ourselves and to be accepted by others. This always leads to conflict when significant others – parents, teachers, clergy, peers – want us to fulfill their purpose, their version of the person we ought to be, rather than the person we are.

From the time I began to develop a mind of my own, my mother and I were in conflict. I recall how I believed that perhaps being Confirmed, i.e., "receive the Holy Spirit" according to the doctrine of my church, I would somehow be empowered to get along better with my mother. Not surprisingly, the benefits of Confirmation and attending Holy Communion only lasted for an hour or two after arriving home. Our "life purposes" for me were obviously at odds, and I was almost thirty–two years old before I broke free of the inner conflict of trying to please both myself and my mother.

During the intervening years, I continued to try to please significant others and to live by the values of my parents and the culture into which I was born. Although I would occasionally break out into some signs of independence, my dominant purpose was to be successful according to the values of others. For this reason, my purpose was relatively powerless. It was not my own.

This orientation was apparent in many areas, but especially in my school work. Because of the need to please, I could not afford to be original and creative, thus risking criticism and rejection. While my technical skills of reading, writing and arithmetic were excellent, I applied them within the boundaries of anticipated approval. Only once, when I was a high school senior, did I evidence any signs of creativity, and that was in writing an essay on a safe subject, my father's dislike of formal dress for attending the opera and other such occasions. Much to my amazement, the humorous essay won second prize in the annual upper school contest, but the glory was short–lived when our English teacher informed us they were the worst set of essays she'd ever seen.

Because of my excellent technical skills, I achieved high scores on the SAT and thus was accepted at the college of my choice. Even this choice, however, was determined by my need to succeed according to parental and cultural values. I had often thought I would like to study architecture, but did not have the courage to apply to a university where such a course was offered.

My college record was average, although I did finally make the dean's list senior year. I had expected to major in math and physics, but after taking an introductory course in psychology sophomore year, decided to change my major to psychology. As I was in the process of making that decision, my father decided to pay me a visit. He had just resigned from a company for which he had worked many years, had not yet signed on with another company, and so had some spare time.

My father had always been totally involved in his work, so that my contact with him was mostly in attending sporting events. He often took me to baseball, hockey and football games, and at one point when I was fourteen, even had me outfitted with a Parker shotgun in hopes that I would like to shoot skeet. I shot the gun only twice – the "kick" was more than I cared to handle. Not to be defeated, my father taught me to drive in his new Cadillac on the way home from the shooting range.

I was pleased and delighted that my father chose to visit me. During his time on campus, we had a discussion about my change in major field of study. He wanted to know why I was making the change, considering that so many good jobs were available for physicists and mathematicians (it was during WWII). I told him that while I was getting reasonably good grades in those courses, I was certainly no whiz, and that I decided that the world was in greater need of understanding human behavior than of technical expertise. I said that I was making the change on the basis of an introductory course in psychology taught by a professor who encouraged my shift by his interesting lectures. Much to my relief, my father did not try to discourage me, but accepted my explanation for changing direction.

Following graduation from college, I once again did what was expected of me: I married a Harvard graduate when he came home from WWII, helped put him through law school (it would never have occurred to me to go to law school myself), had two children, and did volunteer work at church and in the community. I had left my psychology studies behind me after one of my professors had committed suicide following our final exam senior year. What good is psychology if it is no help in solving life's problems?

In marrying my Harvard husband, I did go against my parents' wishes in that he was a Roman Catholic, but other than that, he represented all their values. What I failed to foresee was that he would be married to his career, with me coming along as an assistant. When I divorced him twenty years later, my mother sided with him (my father had since died) and said that the man I next married was "never to darken her door". After she almost died from a stroke, she relented, and the two of them eventually became good friends. She especially liked the martinis he made for her.

Crisis Time

When I had been married for over nine years, living what I have called a powerless purpose, I became depressed with what I experienced as a purposeless and meaningless life. My natural energy was apparently depleted, and I saw no reason to go on. In this seemingly hopeless state, I never considered psychotherapy (memories of that professor's suicide), but turned to my religion, or rather to a remote sense of God. I remembered the words of a seventh grade Sunday school teacher to the effect that God accepted me the way I was, and I was conscious of being very, very tired of trying to live up to expectations, both my own and those of others. I just wanted to be.

With this thought in mind, I went one evening to the old chapel on the grounds of our church, and essentially turned my life over to God, whatever that might mean. It was an extremely frightening process, letting go of being the only person I had known how to be – but it worked. I went home to bed, and when I awoke the next morning, I was full of the energy of being myself, even though I did not yet know that self, and I experienced life as having meaning and purpose, even though I did not have words for the experience. I soon learned that life to be a creative process, that I was meant to be a part of that process, and that the price of admission to the process was to be myself.

Some years later I came to call the sense of purpose I experienced in breaking through from other–directedness to inner–directedness as essential Purpose (with a capital P), the core Purpose for all beings, the Universe, the Cosmos. Pierre Teilhard de Chardin, in his remarkable book THE PHENOM-ENON OF MAN, helped me to articulate this concept in my mind.

Passionate Paths

The next problem, often a very difficult one, is finding our individual purpose, our existential purpose, and applying it in our everyday lives. For me, this has not been a simple matter, in that I have been side–tracked many, many times. While I have been committed in general to communicating the importance of making the shift from powerless to powerful living, I have often done this in less than effective ways.

For example, soon after my crisis experience I followed the traditional practice of enrolling in a graduate course at a seminary as the expected fol-low–up to a "spiritual awakening". I soon came to understand, however, that most (not all) of my professors and fellow students were more interested in the so–called power of patriarchy than in what Riane Eisler (THE CHALICE AND THE BLADE) calls the power of partnership. They also appeared to be more interested in the fine points of religion than in spiritual creativity. A deciding moment for my departure from seminary came in a course on human relations when I asked a classmate why she put up with the faculty's "power over" her, and she replied that soon she would have that power herself. Degrees and ordination seemed to have more to do with power over than power with.

Before I left my seminary education (training?), a classmate introduced me to an interdenominational magazine and movement devoted to a sharing of "faith". It was with this group that I experienced much more spiritual power than at the seminary, although after several years of involvement I once again had to take my departure. My theological views no longer fit their Evangelical Christian approach, and because of my need for intellectual integrity, I was no longer welcome as a member of the editorial board of the magazine. Mean-while, however, I had learned the power of the written word when I had two articles published in the magazine.

Before my split from the evangelical organization, my son's school princi-pal introduced me to the writing of Carl Rogers when he loaned me a copy of ON BECOMING A PERSON. This was for me a thrilling discovery, a psychology which was a fit with my own experiential and intellectual learnings since the crisis experience. It was through this introduction that I became familiar with and a member of the (then American) Association for Humanistic Psychology, eventually attending and giving presentations at its annual meetings, writing articles for its newsletter, serving on the board of directors and briefly as a staff member. I became aware once again of how important the congruency of mind, heart and soul is to the power of purpose. Perspective must change to fit new experience.

When my first marriage ended in the late 1960s, I was faced with the need to earn my own living, and so applied for admission to graduate school. Actually, this proved to be a great relief after many years of less than challenging volunteer work, even though I had a problem in finding ways of following my own interests within required curricula.

By the middle of the first year, it had become clear to me that most of the courses in Applied Psychology were killing my spirit. One of two exceptions was a course in which I was able to choose my own assignments and to lead a seminar on the implications of humanistic psychology for education (a topic new to the students and professor), which proved to be the liveliest class of the year.

At the end of the year I transferred to the department of Adult Education. It was a shift from top–down teaching to partnership learning, where faculty, staff and students formed a learning community. It was during that year that I was able to read extensively on the subject of creativity and also write a paper for a course in Psychology of Adults which was the most powerful piece of writing I had ever done. The professor, to her everlasting credit, had given me permission to write on a subject closest to my heart and in my chosen format. It merited my only A+ in graduate school.

Moving On

Following graduate school I served for one school year as a counselor at a university, but became frustrated with the fact that the students who came to me for help had a limited or distorted view of themselves. Such a view was nearly impossible to change in the brief times I had with them.

With this experience it became clear to me that I was more of an educator than a counselor, and so it was that I accepted a teaching position at a community college the following September. As a psychology teacher in daytime programs and in evening courses with adults, I was able to include my "meaning and purpose" perspective, but not as the primary focus of readings and discussion.

The power of purpose as spiritual commitment was never the centerpiece of classroom learning, which I now believe limited the power of my teaching.

A Major Change

After several years of teaching, my partner and I made a major move to a different country and community, to different lines of work, close to my family and fare removed from his family. He went into remodeling and constructing houses, for which he had good hands–on skills but no business experience, a career so far from his calling and involving so many other problems (such as interest rates at 22%!) that he eventually went bankrupt. Meanwhile I worked in several consecutive low–paying ($5–$7 per hour!) positions as coordinator or director of community agencies, again communicating my perspective to a limited number of co–workers and clients but not as the primary focus of my work. Although I tried to do some writing, I found that concerns about financial problems distracted my thoughts and drained my energy. The power of my purpose was severely depleted.

To recover from years of financial and emotional distress, my partner found it necessary to return to his earlier calling of teaching in our former community, and after fulfilling a work commitment of several months, I joined him. After applying without success for several health education programs for which I was well qualified (more stress!), I was hired at age sixty–four by a large health center to revive a faltering outreach program for seniors.

This was an administrative position but with an important component of offering non–credit classes for older adults on such topics as being "fully alive", an activity much closer to my heart. I continued in this line of work until forcibly retired at age seventy, but not without reporting every year from age sixty–five for a physical exam to be sure I was still functioning adequately, at least at the physical level. My mental state was never tested.

Before my departure from salaried employment, I wrote a booklet for the elderly (THIRD AGE WELLBEING HANDBOOK) which incorporated much of my thinking and which was published with grant funds from a health foundation. Following my so–called retirement, which I have occasionally re-ferred to as getting a new set of tires, I provided content for a CD on the topic of aging and spirituality and later presented the material in booklet form. My power of purpose seemed reasonably strong in these activities, but not yet at full potential.

My most recent sidetrack (or was it?) was in accompanying my husband through several years of health problems and his eventual painful death from leukemia, a terribly distressing experience for both of us. I question whether this stressful time was indeed a sidetrack in that I was compelled to write out a story after his death describing the many missteps in his medical treatment. I had lain awake night after night going over the material in my mind, and finally had to write it out in order to regain my much needed sleep.

When my husband could no longer teach his courses at the community college, I took over for him in several of them, and while I enjoyed the time with the students, not so the preparation, assignments and grading which were time and energy consuming. I have recently turned down an opportunity for teaching more courses to focus fully on writing and hopefully publishing two books. My power of purpose remains in the sharing of ideas and of connections which I have come to believe are crucial to the healing of persons, families, communities, nations and planet.

Concluding Thoughts
(not written in stone)

There comes a time to put thoughts in writing, even though they may be incomplete and subject to change with further explorations and experiences. Following are some of my beliefs and understandings at this point in my life.

- **Purpose and Wholeness**: There is nothing more dangerous than a powerful purpose which originates with a person or group of persons whose psyches are severely damaged or distorted by life experience. The Hitlers, terrorists, violent criminals, and even some politicians of this world are passionately dedicated to destroying human life, often in the name of strange gods or outlandish ideals. Powerful purpose can only be trusted in those committed to healing, wholeness and compassion for person and planet.

- **Purpose and Vocation**: It seems to me that powerful purpose and vocation are closely related, in that we experience personal power only to the extent that we respond to our own inner "callings". Parker J. Palmer, in his book LET YOUR LIFE SPEAK, notes that he even had to let go of being a "good" Quaker in order to listen to his inner voice and experience the power of his vocation. He was thus able to make use of his unique and best talents to contribute to needed reforms in education. Likewise Dawna Markova, in I WILL NOT DIE AN UNLIVED LIFE, *Reclaiming Purpose and Passion*, tells of taking time out to find her true and powerful purpose and vocation. She lives her purpose with passion in her writings and in founding learning communities to help others find their purposeful paths.

• **Purpose and Connection**: Sometimes an admirable and powerful purpose can nevertheless be disconnected from an underlying and unresolved problem, and therefore be less powerful in solving the problem than it might be. An example is MADD (Mothers Against Drunk Drivers), which aims to keep drunks from behind the wheel of moving vehicles. The members are highly motivated, in that they have lost children to accidents caused by drivers under the influence of alcohol. They fail to connect, however, with the underlying causes of such behavior, a challenge which is left to other persons and organizations.

• **Purpose and Creativity**: Since creativity appears to be the way of the Cosmos, and since we are expressions of the Cosmos, our natural way of being is one of creative process, a way of meaning and purpose. Many years ago, psychologist and educator Clark Moustakas wrote a book entitled CREATIVITY AND CONFORMITY, and since then many other writers have pointed out how our need to conform blocks our ability to live a creative life. As children, most of us have no choice but to conform if we want to survive to adulthood, but we fail to recognize how important it is to become our own creative persons, acting from our most heartfelt motivation and expressing our unique talents as our gift to life. Only then can we fuel our purpose with the power of the universe, the natural energy, consciousness, and compassion which is available to us when we become our real selves, living from the depth of our own souls. The healing of ourselves and our planet depends on our participation in and personal expression of the Creative Spirit of all that is.

Chapter 10

IN SEARCH OF WHOLENESS

Self and the Inner Connection

Self–expression is the primary sacrament of the universe. Whatever you deeply feel demands to be given form and released. Take supernovas as your models. When they had filled themselves with riches, they exploded in a vast cosmic celebration of their work. What would you have done? Would you have had the courage to flood the universe with your riches? Or would you have talked yourself out of it by pleading that you were too shy? It's the same with human celebration, generosity, and creativity: try to bottle them up and you only get neurosis and destruction.

Brian Swimme,
THE UNIVERSE IS A GREEN DRAGON

I was blessed with a family where it felt safe to be myself, so my dividedness did not begin at home. But I did not feel safe at school, despite my capacity to act the role of a "successful" and "popular" student, words I put in quotation marks because the role felt so fraudulent to me. While I played my onstage part, my true self hid out backstage, fearful that the world would crush its deepest values and beliefs, its fragile hopes and yearnings.

Parker J. Palmer,
A HIDDEN WHOLENESS:
The Journey Toward an Undivided Life

$\mathcal{R}$ecently a discussion with a long–time friend centered on the difference between perfection and wholeness. He was raised in a conservative religious family, and at age sixteen he was deeply concerned with the goal of being perfect in order to be acceptable to God. His greatest fear was the possibility of being rejected by God. In working towards his goal, he studied for the ministry at a conservative Christian seminary, became an ordained clergyman – and eventually left the Church. He gave up on trying to be perfect, an unattainable goal, in favor of wholeness.

Also known to me are several women who likewise have aimed for perfection in various aspects of their lives: how they dress, the way they keep their homes and raise their children, and in over–commitment to their work life. It seems that for these women, their perfectionism is an attempt to avoid rejection by parents and teachers in their childhood years and by family, friends and colleagues as adults.

Their primary concern is to avoid rejection by other human beings, not God.

The problem is that we are not now and never will be perfect human beings, and if our focus is on perfecting our own behavior, we relate to others at a performance level rather than heart to heart or soul to soul. For example, if a child is accidentally injured, the caregiver's first thought is his or her own failure in caring for the child rather than what the child is experiencing. Another example: if a guest drops in unexpectedly, the host's primary concern is the condition of the house rather than the comfort of the guest. That home needs a sign on the wall reading "If you want to see me, come any time; if you want to see my house, make an appointment."

Wholeness, in contrast to perfection, is a matter of accepting ourselves and others in our entirety, "warts and all". We acknowledge our failures as well as our successes, our fears as well as our joys, and we relate to others out of our imperfection. If we serve as role models at all, it is as imperfect human beings, not as models of perfection.

In our search for wholeness we often need to seek healing for past painful experiences and harmful transgressions. Millions of people the world over turn to psychotherapy and other forms of life–changing methods to deal with problems of inner trauma and conflict. Not only is this a personal issue, but it becomes very much a political issue when persons who fail to acknowledge and address such inner conflicts act them out on families, friends, communities, and even nations and the world. Alice Miller has written about Hitler's acting out of unacknowledged, unhealed pain and anger, with obvious disastrous results. We see dreadful examples every day at every level of society of persons acting out their fears, pains, angers and traumas.

From time to time I have been moved to write about the importance of the search for wholeness. Following is an article I wrote almost thirty years ago.

Crossovers

WHAT THE WORLD NEEDS NOW are more and more "crossovers". By crossover I mean a crossing over in consciousness from trying to be someone we are not to letting ourselves be who we are; from trying to be best in comparison to other people to aiming for excellence in terms of our own combination of abilities; from perceiving ourselves as victims of life to experiencing ourselves as expressions of life; from driving ourselves as though we are machines to valuing ourselves as living organisms; from using others and the environment for our own ends to interacting creatively with others and the environment so we can all be winners.

This kind of crossover is known by many other names. Ernest Lawrence Rossi, a clinical psychologist who has worked extensively with college students in Southern California, speaks of the "breakout heuristic" as a creative process through which his student–clients make such a shift in consciousness in the process of psychotherapy. They have come to him for help because of a loss of motivation, direction, and meaning in their lives. They often perceive themselves as sick because they no longer seem able to function in a normal manner. The therapist's task is to support and encourage the clients in the process of self–discovery and self–acceptance, the shift from outer–directedness to inner–directedness, and to effective self–expression in relationship to other people and the environment – the beginning of the most exciting and satisfying journey any of us can ever take.

Several years ago, when I was a member of the counseling staff at a Canadian university, a young man came to see me to find out what courses he should take. While he was a brilliant student, he had given up on his math and engineering courses because he was unable to force himself to attend classes or do his assignments, and he was sleeping much of the time. He thought that perhaps a shift to a general arts program would help, and he wanted me to tell him what courses he would like best. Needless to say, I declined the invitation with the explanation that I couldn't possibly know what would please and interest him, and then did what I could to assist him in making his own choices.

This proved to be a waste of time. He was so out of touch with his own feelings and opinions that his own choices were merely wild guesses, and within a few weeks he was as bored and depressed as in his previous program. He continued to come to see me every week or two, and during these sessions I learned that he had long ago given up having any opinions of his own (even as to what movie to see) for fear of being rejected by other people. He was the perfect human chameleon, able to take on the color of any person or group of people with whom he might associate, and he had lost himself in the process.

He was sufficiently concerned about his condition that he was seeing a psychiatrist every week, and yet he continued to drop in to see me at the counseling office every week or ten days. All I had to offer him was the conviction and reassurance that he had a unique core or center or self that was waiting to be released whenever he was ready to take a chance on it. Eventually he accepted an invitation to attend a day–long "awareness" session at our home, and on that occasion he experienced some *feelings* for the first time in years. The following week he dismissed the episode as an accident or a figment of his imagination, although I encouraged him to accept it as a sign of life within.

School ended about that time. He returned to his home in Toronto, and I left the university to accept a teaching position at a community college some distance away. The following fall, when we were several weeks into the new semester, I received a telephone call which was unexpected and quite exciting. It was the same student, reporting that he had found his way, was thrilled with his sense of direction, and was enjoying the stimulation and challenge of his new program of courses.

I recently read a book by Derrick Jensen entitled WALKING ON WATER: Reading, Writing and Revolution (Chelsea Green Publishing Company, 2003, 2005). The book relates to the search for wholeness in terms of helping students to find themselves and their passion as the primary purpose of education. It reminded me of two short pieces I wrote on education, the first about thirty years ago, the second more recently.

Learning As Creative Process

THERE ARE PRIMARILY TWO KINDS of learning, two dimensions to our education, and neither can be ignored if we are to become effective and fulfilled members of society. One dimension is the acquisition of skills, the development of existing potential and abilities in such a way that we are able to interact more extensively with our environment. Such skills might include anything from cake decorating to typing and shorthand, piano–playing to electrical wiring, writing up case studies to speaking a foreign language, and so on. All require a measure of precision in terms of physical dexterity or in the use of symbols or observational skills or other such abilities, usually in some combination.

The second dimension of learning has to do with the development of our capacity for inner awareness of ourselves, others, and the world around us in such a way that we can interact effectively and creatively with all aspects of our environment, both people and things. Such creativity is only possible when we are in touch with our own thoughts and feelings, respect ourselves and others as persons, experience ourselves and the world around us in an honest and realistic way, and freely choose and act upon our own values. We must also be flexible enough to be open to new experience and to change our views, values and behavior when new information warrants such a change. This kind of learning can be difficult in a society where there is so much pressure towards conformity.

The acquisition of skills without growth in personal awareness or awareness without skills are both basically inadequate and unsatisfying ways of functioning. If we have acquired only skills, we will function much like machines and will experience little of the aliveness which comes with interacting creatively with our environment. If on the other hand we acquire only personal awareness, we will have a very limited experience of such creative interaction because we are lacking in skills with which to communicate or express our creativity in relationship to the world around us.

Effective education or learning occurs when we grow as tall as we can both in terms of skills appropriate to our own potential and of expanding our awareness and the freedom to interact with our world, a life–enhancing creative process.

Schools: Factories Or Flowerbeds?

MANY WRITERS HAVE HELPED US to understand that how we view our world, our society, and our fellow human beings determines how we treat ourselves, other human beings, and our planet. If we see ourselves and others, including our children, primarily as cogs in the social machine and our planet as a way of servicing that machine, we will treat people and planet accordingly. If on the other hand we perceive persons as souls with unique potentials and a need to give expression to those potentials in creative and compassionate living, we will treat them in quite a different way. Likewise if we perceive our planet earth as a living organism of which we are a part, we will treat it with caring and respect.

Nowhere is our view of human nature more important than in our schools and in our approach to education. If we accept the viewpoint of many who see our children as finding their purpose in fulfilling the needs of the commercial machine which our society has become, we will accept the idea that children must all pass tests on the same content presented in the same way at the same grade levels as proof of adequate education.

However, if we see our children each as one–of–a–kind with a unique neurological makeup and particular gifts to be developed as their contribution to a healthy society, we will opt for a much more creative approach to education. We will seek to prepare them to give their own best and to enjoy the learning process. At this time of crisis, not only in our particular society but all over the world, which philosophy will we adopt as the basis of our educational institutions?

Flowerbed Philosophy

Children are viewed as unique combinations of potential talents, maturing at different times and in different ways, and functioning in a variety of learning modes. With this in mind, we need to provide a nurturing, creative and resource–rich approach to education which includes *all* children as valuable members of the learning community. Possible problems: difficulty in holding their own and being true to their own nature in a society which at present often fails to value what they have to offer.

Factory Philosophy

Children are viewed as needing to be molded into what parents, teachers and society want them to be without regard for the special make–up of each child. Their success is to be measured by how well they stack up against external demands, which justifies across the board testing for all. Those who are "developmentally challenged" or whose talents are not valued are considered failures in the competitive success–oriented approach. Probable problems: exclusion from the learning community through no fault of their own, resulting in self–alienation and alienation from others, shame, anger and frustration, often resulting in mental health problems, addictions, and even criminal activity.

On which view of the child do we choose to base our approach to education?

Having raised the issue of mental health, this seems to be a good place to include something about depression as loss of spirit and the search for wholeness. I wrote the following piece in 1998 to include in adult education courses offered through a health center and a public library.

Depression And The Loss Of Performance Power

IN OUR PERFORMANCE ORIENTED SOCIETY, we often fail to realize how much energy it takes to keep on performing up to expectations – our own, others', or perceived others' – day in and day out, year after year. We also fail to recognize that the onset of depression is often the consequence of running out of performance power.

I am not speaking here of situational depression which is the result of painful events and losses which require grieving and reorientation over a period of time. I am concerned rather with the kind of depression which does not appear to be the result of some external cause, but is a deep internal sense of hopelessness about life itself with no way out of the darkness. The medical response to this condition is almost always a prescription for an anti–depressant.

From a more holistic perspective, such depression may be a blessing in disguise (as was the case for Parker J. Palmer, LET YOUR LIFE SPEAK, and Dean Ornish, LOVE AND SURVIVAL). It may be a call to give up living in the performance mode in which we expend tremendous amounts of energy in order to gain the admiration, respect, acceptance and love from others, and to move into living in the creative mode in which we activate our natural spiritual energy.

This may sound simplistic, which in a way it is, but it is certainly not simple in terms of what it takes to let go of a way of life which is familiar in order to risk a way of living from which we have long been separated. It often takes a psycho–spiritual crisis to push us over the brink into the unexpected aliveness of living out the direction of our own souls rather than for the approval of others. At some point the fear of loss of self must become greater than the fear of the loss of others. Performance power must be replaced with soul power, the creative energy of the universe which requires faithfulness to our own uniqueness and respect for the uniqueness and self–direction of others.

Strange as it may seem, it is in foregoing the need for the approval of others in favor of deep respect for self and others that honest love and intimacy become possible. This is not to say that we necessarily respect the beliefs, values and behaviors of all other people, but that we honor their unique personhood and recognize that each of us is at some stage of development. For some, spiritual development may have become arrested due to life circumstances or fear or ignorance, while for others growth is an ongoing creative process.

From this perspective, depression is the natural consequence of blocking out our own inner experience in order to be "acceptable" to others. We kill our own spirit as we deny our own souls and fail to be who we are.

Last evening I pulled a book off the shelf which I had read several years ago, SINGING AT THE TOP OF OUR LUNGS by Claudia Bepko and Jo–Ann Krestan (HarperCollins Publishers, 1993). The authors tell of a number of women in their search for wholeness and aliveness, and as well describe five primary patterns these women have followed in expressing their passions: Lovers, Artists, Leaders, Innovators, and Visionaries. Creative self–expression is the issue in every case. This focus reminded me of an article I wrote with an emphasis on dancing and wholeness.

A Question Of Inner Dancing

HAVING BEEN MARRIED TWICE TO non–dancers, the first time for twenty years and the second for over thirty–five, I wonder now (in my late seventies) why I never realized how much I would miss dancing as a vital aspect of life. Actually, I did not know in advance that neither one would be interested in dancing once we were married. In the courting stage, both danced, although certainly not with wild abandon. Both did go dancing once in a long while during the course of our married lives, but only when fortified with several martinis.

What I had failed to understand was that, with both these men, dancing was a self–conscious performance rather than a form of self–expression. My second husband had enjoyed square dancing, sometimes as a caller, before I met him. That had provided good exercise and the safety of pre–designated structure without the risk of improvisation. I had square danced occasionally in my earlier life and considered it good exercise, but was not much turned on by the formality of it. As for the polka, which we danced at his daughter's Croatian wedding, it was rather fun and again good exercise, but at least in our case included no variations, no creative improvisation.

During my high school years, I had been quite envious of classmates whose dates were into jitterbugging. I thought it would be great fun, but unfortunately was never paired up with boys who were good at that form of dance.

As for ballroom dancing, in which I had been trained beginning in seventh grade, I can recall only two occasions when I danced with men who were superb dancers. Both were friends of my first husband, one of whom married my college roommate. In his case, he commented (seriously or in jest?) that he would have to choose between dance and the ministry as a career, and he chose the latter. That was undoubtedly a gain for the church, but in my opinion a great loss for the dancing community. As for the second man, I can't remember who he was except that we went to a dance with him and his wife, and that my brief time on the dance floor with him was a special experience.

What I failed to realize until recent years is that my own inner–dancing, that sense of rhythm and joy when one is in touch with the dance of one's soul, slowly began to fade away when paired with a non–dancer. I also began to put on weight, to become "heavy". There were a few occasions which should have brought this issue to my attention, such as an unusual experience one Sunday afternoon in the town of Davenport on the California coast.

My husband and I had placed an ad in the local newspaper offering our services for modest fees in assisting clients in remodeling and redecorating to reflect their own needs and tastes. A young man responded with a request to help him decorate a tiny cabin in the sand dunes in which he planned to make a movie. We could see that this would likely not be financially rewarding, but it would be an adventure, so we agreed to help him. On the return from visiting his film site, he offered to treat us to a beer or two (big fee substitute!), which is how we found ourselves in the little bar in Davenport.

In addition to the bar, there were three or four small tables and a juke box. We sat at one of the tables and placed our order, wine for me and beer for the other two. We had just settled ourselves when a grizzled old guy with no front teeth, one of five or six men at the bar, asked me, the only female in the place, to dance. He even offered us a round of drinks in exchange for the privilege.

I accepted his offer, and soon found myself dancing with each of the other men at the bar. A couple of them spoke only Spanish, but that was no hindrance on the dance floor. One even chose a flamenco on the juke box, so of course there was much clicking of heels. Every time the old gentleman with no teeth (do I dare call him geezer?) took his turn, he ordered us another round of drinks. We finally had to call a halt to his generosity or dance fee, depending on how you choose to look at it, and I danced with him one last time without the booze.

What an afternoon, with me the "belle of the bar" so to speak! I've never forgotten how much I enjoyed that experience in a little bar on the coast and wonder whether I'll ever again have such an opportunity. It was so informal, so spontaneous, that I thoroughly enjoyed the music, the men, and the dancing

My two companions were content to sit and watch the "entertainment".

Now, many years later, I feel an urgent need to re–connect with my inner–dancing, and am wondering where to begin. I am on my own now, my long–time partner having died several months ago, and I believe that such a reconnection is important to my health as well as my creativity. I understand that I can dance alone, but I prefer dancing with a partner in a way that body and soul are moving to a common rhythm and with a sense of connection. I look forward to where my search will take me, hopefully to the inner/outer dance connection.

Chapter 11

HEALTH, ILLNESS, DEATH

Beyond the Symptoms

We are healthy when we are in touch with our rhythms and risking to live them. At an everyday level this means knowing the what and when of our needs – sleep, companionship, adventure, solitude, whatever – and forming our lives so these things can be honored. In the musical metaphor, the therapeutic alliance is a shared commitment to honoring these notes and how they wish to be patterned.

Medicine is having to face squarely the specter of death, both as a symbol – the fact of limitation, death as the surrender of a godly image – and death in a very literal sense – the fact that death is a part of life.

In its day, medicine's heroic image of victory over darkness brought immensely rich rewards. Initially, giving up this image may feel like a major sacrifice. But a larger vision of medicine, while certainly demanding more of us, will ultimately be both more fulfilling and more health–giving.

Charles M. Johnston, M.D.,
THE CREATIVE IMPERATIVE:
A Four–Dimensional Theory of Human Growth
and Planetary Evolution.

*W*ith four score years of living behind me, I have become much more aware of the part that health or lack of it can play in our lives. As a child, I was aware of the illness and deaths of my great-grandmother and my grandfather, both of whom I knew as part of my life during summers on the East Coast. Their deaths, however, made little impact on my life.

That was certainly not the case when my little sister died of a ruptured appendix after a lingering infection. I was fifteen at the time, and she was ten years my junior. To say that it was an extremely emotional experience is an under-statement, and it was complicated by the fact that my brother and I (he was five years younger than me) were not allowed to discuss our feelings about what had happened. What's more, my mother permitted no pictures of the child in our home for ten years, and apparently never forgave a doctor for failing to diagnose the problem.

Other than my sister's illness, and the case of a classmate's sister who died of tuberculosis, sickness was something from which one recovered without undue consequences. Personally, I never had any serious illness, unless one would consider it serious that I came down with the flu six hours before the sophomore prom, my first formal dance. My date stopped by with my corsage on his way to the dance. It was a disaster of sorts, but hardly life-threatening.

During my middle years, a friend and neighbor developed leukemia, and after a lingering illness, died at the young age of thirty-eight. Of course it was a shock, but again it was an isolated event, certainly not an everyday occurrence. Life went on, as did the friendship with his widow and children.

Much closer to home was the death of my father when he was sixty-six and I was only forty. He had been a heavy smoker for many years and eventually developed emphysema. There was not the kind of treatment available then as is offered now, and when he acquired a lung infection, he entered the hospital for the last time. Through a strange set of circumstances, I was able to be with him during the last three days of his life as he drifted in and out of consciousness. At one point he asked about Winny, and I did not know what he meant until I read in the paper that Winston Churchill was seriously ill. As fate would have it, my father and Churchill, the man he most admired, died on the same day.

In my later years, there have of course been many more losses, including the deaths of family members including my mother at ninety–three and my younger brother at fifty–seven. I regret that I wasn't with my mother at the time of her dying. I had been with her for several days in the previous week, then traveled to California to stay with my granddaughter while my daughter visited her grandmother, finally returning to work in Canada. I remind myself, however, that I saw to it that my mother remained at home as she wished. Her doctor had refused to treat her unless she went into the hospital, which meant finding another doctor who would see her at home and also arranging for hospice care. She died in her own bed as she wished.

The death of my brother on the ski slopes in Switzerland came as a terrible shock to my mother, who had now outlived two of her children .His death did not mean much to me because we had lived continents apart, both geographically and in terms of our values. I traveled to Monaco with my mother, who was legally blind and needed a traveling companion, for my brother's funeral, and realized at that time that my brother's friends knew him much better than I did. Only recently while in France for a nephew's wedding did I experience long–buried hurt at my brother's rejection of me, and at the same time experience healing in special times with his sons and several of his friends.

The most difficult time for me was the illness and dying of my husband. So many things went wrong during his treatment for leukemia that I lay awake many nights after his death reliving the whole process. I finally had to write out the following story in order to let go of night after night of reliving the process. I need to add that I have had some qualms about including this very personal story, but decided that Ralph would want it told if it can be of any help to others.

Story Of An Illness

ON OCTOBER 3, 1998, RALPH took his blood pressure reading on a home monitor and found it to be unusually high. He was concerned enough to go that day to a walk–in clinic, where the doctor on duty immediately prescribed medication. Ralph took the doctor's warning seriously and began taking the prescribed medicine as instructed.

Not long after going on the prescribed medication, Ralph became impotent, but when read information from publications about blood pressure issues stating that his medication could be causing the problem, he dismissed it as of no value. Nothing more was said about the problem, although he must have been distressed by the situation.

The following March (1999), Ralph injured his knee in a home accident. He went to Emergency where a doctor told him that it would heal in a couple of weeks. When Ralph told him that he could not walk on that leg because it simply collapsed, the doctor gave him a pair of crutches, but failed to teach him how to use them. On reaching home, Ralph fell backwards trying to go up the steps, but fortunately without further injury.

Ignoring suggestions to see his family doctor, Ralph saw only a chiropractor for three weeks until he also told Ralph to see his family doctor. His doctor immediately made an appointment for Ralph with an orthopedic surgeon, who revealed that the problem was a detached muscle that would never recover without surgery. An operation was scheduled for early May. A pre–op blood test showed that Ralph's white blood count was below normal, but the surgery went ahead as planned.

While the operation went well, infection set in soon afterwards, and after several trips to Emergency to have the incision drained, the surgeon decided that it would have to be re–opened and allowed to heal from the inside out. This process took several months of antibiotics and daily changes of dressings.

Meanwhile, Ralph was sent to a hematologist about the blood problem. There he was told that he had a slightly enlarged spleen and was given a bone marrow test, but was given no explanation for the white count problem and no treatment.

Since the only change in Ralph's lifestyle between a normal white count and a below normal count was taking the blood pressure medication, it occurred to us to ask the pharmacist whether a lowered white count could be a side effect of the medication. Much to the pharmacist's own surprise, he found that in a small percentage of patients, there was indeed such a problem. Ralph passed this information on to his doctors, who apparently considered it of no consequence. Eventually his family doctor (a different one than previously) did agree to change the prescription, but the new one proved to have the same side effect as the earlier one. Ralph took the medication for three years in spite of the possible problem.

Ralph continued to have regular blood tests and a yearly bone marrow test. His white count remained steady at the below normal level and the bone marrow tests indicated that, while the marrow continued to produce blood, it was diminishing in quality. As previously, no treatment was indicated while regular monitoring was maintained.

In December of 2001, while Ralph was out of the country for the holidays, he developed a very serious sinus infection and began to bleed profusely from his nose whenever he blew it. He also experienced soreness in the location of his spleen at this time. He decided to wait to see his doctor on his return to Canada, so received no treatment while he was away.

On Ralph's return home in early January 2002, he went for a blood test which he had skipped in December, and soon had a call from his doctor with the distressing news that his platelet level had dropped drastically. His doctor had contacted the hematologist about a possible platelet transfusion, but was told that it would be useless as it would last only a day or two. No further action was recommended at that time.

Ralph was sufficiently concerned about this new problem that he researched the platelet issue in medical books, on the Internet, and with his brother, a retired doctor. A number of possible treatments were recommended, with the removal of the spleen high on the list. His brother told him that it was a relatively simple surgery and often solved the problem. Ralph passed this information on to his doctors, who ignored it as a solution although they offered no alternative.

On March 28, 2002, Ralph went to see his dentist because of a swollen upper left gum. It surrounded a dead tooth which had been left in because it was causing no trouble. At this time the dentist said that he did not want to alarm Ralph, but thought that the gum might be cancerous, and made an appointment for him to see a dentist specializing in gum problems. The opinion was confirmed, and Ralph was sent back to his dentist for the removal of two teeth and a biopsy of the gum. The gum bled for a week, which was a bad sign, and the biopsy report came back confirming the presence of leukemia cells.

At the same time, Ralph developed a strange red rash all over his arms and back and was sent to a dermatologist, who took two biopsies. It took several weeks for the lab report to come back, by which time the rash had disappeared. The report offered no explanation for the rash.

On April 12, Ralph went to Emergency (on the advice of his gum special-ist) to get immediate attention for the problem, and then on April 16 saw his hematologist and had x–rays taken of the gum. At this time he was diagnosed with "slow–moving" acute myeloid leukemia, which was most discouraging. He also had several further appointments with his dentist and specialist relat-ed to gum problems.

On May 8 Ralph met again with his hematologist, who decided on ra-diation for the gum and made an appointment with the radiologist, whom Ralph saw on May 14. He reported to the cancer center on June 7 to have a face shield made, and was supposed to begin four daily radiation treatments on June 10. However, the doctor forgot to schedule the treatments, and with the help of Ralph's very supportive social worker, the treatments were re–sched-uled for June 20.

For some unexplained reason, the radiologist changed the number of treatments from four to twelve. All went well for the first nine treatments, after which the inside of Ralph's cheek became burned. He saw the radiolo-gist about the problem before the twelfth and last treatment and questioned whether he should go ahead with it. The radiologist said it was not a problem and that he should have it. The result was a worse burn and then a serious infection. His last radiation treatment was on July 8, by which time his mouth was so sore and blistered that his diet was severely restricted to soft foods and liquids.

During the six months since the platelet problem, Ralph had continued teaching his classes at the community college, seeing his counseling clients, and carrying on a normal social life, including a trip to my sixtieth high school reunion in May. By that time he was tiring very easily and restricted his activities to those which meant the most to him.

We had planned to leave early in July for our usual summer visit with family and friends in California, but because of the delay in the radiation treatments and Ralph's subsequent mouth infection, we were unable to depart until July 22. The hematologist ordered a blood transfusion to bolster Ralph's energy while we were away, and we left with a big supply of antibiotics for the mouth infection, although they seemed to have little or no effect.

We had a wonderful time for eight days, but by then Ralph's upper gum had swollen down over his front teeth, and he decided he had to return to Canada to deal with the problem. We left California on July 31, four weeks short of our intended visit. On his return, Ralph had appointments with the radiologist and with dentists at the hospital, resulting in more medications; continued to see the hematologist on a regular basis; and on August 8 had blood and platelet transfusions.

At this time he also began complementary treatments (Reiki, therapeutic touch, meditation, etc.) at a center for cancer patients and their families. He was familiar with the writings of the Simontons, Lawrence LeShan, Michael Lerner and others, and practiced visualization on his own. He did not follow a specialized diet, but we had already cut down our meat consumption before his illness.

On September 3, Ralph resumed his teaching at the community college, and on September 5 he had another blood transfusion. On September 13, we traveled to another city to spend the week–end with close friends for Ralph's seventy–ninth birthday. While he tired easily, he very much enjoyed this time of closeness and caring.

On the evening of September 15, Ralph developed a dangerously high fever and uncontrollable shaking. At 3 a.m. on the 16th, we called the ambulance to take him to Emergency. He was duly treated with antibiotics and Tylenol, and sent home about 8:30 a.m. That was a terrible mistake. He became even worse on the night of the 16th, so I called the ambulance again, and this time the doctor had the good sense to admit him to the hospital. He was so ill that he subsequently could not even remember the first few days of the two weeks that he was hospitalized.

Although still very weak, he recovered enough to be sent home. The special antibiotics administered in the hospital had helped to heal his mouth completely, including the swelling of his gums, for the first time in over two months. By this time, he had no choice but to give up his teaching assignments at the college.

Ever since his leukemia diagnosis in the spring, Ralph had been considering chemotherapy as a possible treatment choice. His hematologist warned him of the potential pain and problems, but agreed to go along with Ralph's decision to undergo the treatment. Thus it was that Ralph re–entered the hospital on October 22 (someone forgot to call him about coming in on the 21st), and underwent five days of chemotherapy. All went well for that first week, with no side effects.

At the beginning of Ralph's second week, when he began maintenance procedures of whole blood and platelet transfusions and antibiotics, the situation began to worsen dramatically. The platelet level never improved. The arm in which a pic line had been installed for administering the drugs and transfusions became infected and very swollen and painful. The line was removed and he was sent to another hospital (as previously) to have a line inserted in the other arm. Over the period of three weeks he had x–rays and ultrasounds, and because of internal bleeding which might have clotted in his bladder, underwent a terribly painful procedure of having a catheter inserted in his urinary tract. This resulted in agonizing spasms as his bladder attempted to expel the catheter. He was given anti–spasm medication, which gave only a little relief.

Eventually Ralph's stomach could no longer tolerate food. He began intravenous feedings, but was obviously losing ground and finding the struggle to survive more and more difficult. By this time, I was spending the night in his room (at his request), and only going home for a few hours each day. I found that being with him during such a painful and stressful journey was almost more than I could bear.

On the morning of November 17, the doctor came in and asked Ralph's daughter and myself if we wanted the treatment continued or simply to make Ralph as comfortable as possible. By this time, Ralph had not responded to us for several days and appeared to be exhausted, so we chose the latter. Morphine was administered every half hour until Ralph died early that evening, surrounded by his caring family. The image of his gasping for his last breaths and looking twenty years older than he had looked three weeks earlier continues to haunt my mind. I know without any question that we are not meant to die this way.

Ralph's wishes were carried out according to his instructions, with no "heroic measures" during his last days, his body cremated, and his ashes scattered over the river near his childhood home (although we had a bit of a problem finding a spot where the river wasn't frozen over). We celebrated his life in three gatherings, two in Canada and one in California. We miss him.

Thoughts And Questions

Physical/medical Issues

I have agonized in the intervening three months since Ralph's death over questions as to why, when the doctors had no explanation for his lowered white count, they did not at least consider the information from the pharmacist. I also wonder why Ralph himself did not press the issue when so many alternatives in blood pressure medication are available which indicate no such side effect.

I have agonized, too, over why no attention was paid to the possible causes of the severe drop in platelet count, when considerable information was available from several sources. Why did neither the doctors nor Ralph push for a second opinion about the spleen issue from an internist or a surgeon? It seems as though the problem is a closed system rather than an open process in which communication can flow freely between various specialties and sources of information. While each health provider was caring and well–informed within his/her own area of expertise, there seemed to be no creative interaction with other areas. Surely there must be a better way.

Psychological/spiritual Issues

Even though Ralph had been a teacher of psychology and a counselor for many years, he seemed to have a need to be "wise" and adequate, sharing nothing of his own fears and anxieties during his last months. It was only after his death, when I read something he had written a month or so after his leukemia diagnosis, that I became aware of how very anxious he was. He said that "Both the words leukemia and chemotherapy have for me strong danger connotations, and I am anxious – some days more than others."

Of course it is very normal to be anxious under such circumstances, but unusual for someone so aware of the benefits of psychotherapy to keep such fears and anxieties to himself. Questions: Was it Ralph's need to be the wise and strong counselor which prevented him from voicing his deepest fears, even though he had many close and caring persons in his life? Was it an overpowering feeling of vulnerability unhealed from childhood trauma (of which there were many) that caused him to show only strength?

Two messages about Ralph's being had been especially distressing when he was young: first, that his body, especially his sexuality, could not be trusted and must be controlled at any cost. His mother had warned him that if he "played with himself" (easy to do with one's hands in pockets of overalls!), he would turn out like the village idiot. She had also frightened him terribly when she found him and a little neighbor girl using the outhouse together after school as though it were a major sin. A third incident was a mortifying accident, which happened in school when the teacher did not allow him to go to the washroom. A resulting puddle on the floor caused much laughter by the other children.

Another area of distress was Ralph's supposed lack of intelligence, especially when compared to his two older brothers. His father trashed his labor–saving inventions around the farm as signs of laziness, and while praising the two older boys who were heading for medical and missionary careers, made it clear that he thought Ralph would come to no good end. A counselor informed Ralph on the basis of an I.Q. test that he was not university material, and Ralph failed a course (psychology) and thus his first year at university. He went on to receive his B. A. and to graduate study, becoming a pioneer in the mental health field.

It does seem as though in his later years and at the emotional or spiritual level, Ralph trusted neither his body nor his intelligence and was somehow trying to prove himself in both areas. It may be, too, that his sense of worth continued to depend on the acceptance and admiration of others, even though he had well–developed talents in many areas and had been of great help to many people. If so, such a lack of a personal sense of worth may have contributed to the weakening of his immune system. This in no way saying that he was responsible for his illness, but rather that our cultural ignorance as related to the body/mind connection is the problem which requires urgent and extensive research.

Concluding Thoughts

In a current issue of YES! Magazine, there is an extensive focus on the effect of toxins in the environment on our health. I certainly agree with this assessment of the situation, but I regret that there is little or no mention of the effect of the toxins of unhealed trauma, destructive beliefs and values, and unexpressed emotions on our "inner environment". There appears to be no simplistic single cause for any human illness, and our tendency to take a linear rather than open systems, process approach to health care is, in my opinion, disastrous.

It appears to be absolutely essential that we establish open lines of communication between the various health care providers as well as with those experiencing illness and their families. I also believe that we must move from what I call restrictive, conformist modes of living to open, creative approaches in all aspects of our lives, a matter of saying yes to life, if we are to have strong immune systems. Self–consistency is not a static way of being, but involves creative change as we open ourselves to emotional healings and new understandings. The creative way is the way of the cosmos, the universe, and our planet, and we reject it at our peril.

Since the title of this chapter is HEALTH, ILLNESS, DEATH, a natural follow–up is a consideration of what, if anything, is our experience after death. A recent discussion by a panel of six persons on Larry King's program addressing this issue was interesting in its diversity of beliefs and opinions. The panel consisted of a Fundamentalist Evangelical clergyman, a Roman Catholic priest, a Jewish rabbi, a retired Muslim doctor (all men), a well–known writer on spiritual issues, and a president of a society of atheists (both women). They ranged in their beliefs from rigid to questioning, more of the former than the latter.

The program brought to mind an article I wrote which was published in the Santa Cruz Sentinel (August 4, 2001) and which seems appropriate for inclusion here.

Putting Trust In Doctrine Or Life?

IN AN ARTICLE ABOUT PROBLEMS with the U. S. Navy chaplaincy program (Santa Cruz Sentinel, July 21, 2001), lawyer Art Schultcz is described as representing a number of chaplains in a lawsuit against the Navy. He is quoted as saying that when dealing with life–and–death situations, "Everyone wonders what happens when you die, and religion has the answer." The question is, which answer?

There are as many different descriptions of what happens as there are religions and various perspectives within religions. Hindus, Buddhists, Muslims, Mormons, Roman Catholics, Protestant Christians, etc., give widely varying descriptions of what lies beyond life on earth. Of course not one of them is based on factual knowledge; all are the imagined versions of what happens after death as proclaimed by religion founders and followers to satisfy their own need to continue living.

There are also those who insist that death is the end, period, but their position is not based on fact either. Then there are some, such as the Unitarian–Universalists, who offer no set doctrine and leave it to their members to believe whatever they want.

So what is the real issue here? Are some people so anxious about whether they can continue living in some form that they are willing to accept whatever version of life after death that their particular religion offers? Are there some who are so trusting in the creative life process that they are willing to wait and see? This seems to be the crux of the matter. Many, perhaps most people, appear to need a definite answer, while others are open to all possibilities.

Personally, I choose to wait and see, since I don't trust the imaginations of various religionists to give me an accurate picture of what is to come. I choose to place my trust in life itself rather than in belief systems about the nature of life, death, God and human beings – belief systems based on the thoughts of many different persons of widely divergent cultures throughout history.

I believe passionately, not in a set doctrine, but that the time has come for us to acknowledge that no person and no religion has a final revelation about what lies beyond death. We human beings are in process and need to keep open to new experiences and new understanding of the nature of things if we are to survive as a species on our planet earth.

So where am I now on this question of life after death? Since writing the previous article, my husband of many years and several dear friends have died,

and I myself am eighty years old. Just this morning I read in the paper a quote from a heart specialist that anything over eighty is "a crapshoot", which warns that my days are numbered.

Am I ready to die? Of course not. I have much more work to do and a loving family and friends that I do not care to leave. However, I do recognize that sooner or later (I prefer later) I, too, will leave this life on earth. If I have any hope for something more, it is because I yearn for completing relationships with many who have gone before: my little sister, my brother, my parents, my husband and many friends. I long for an intimacy that I lacked with some of them in this lifetime, a wholeness in relationship which is ultimately fulfilling.

Chapter 12

THE CREATIVE WAY

Perspectives at Four Score Years

To reclaim our full power as creative beings we must expand our way of thinking and living to consider both nature and technology, head and heart, the directive and the uncertain, dark and light. We need to recapture the sense of wonder we knew as a child and blend it with the passion, the sense of responsibility and the ability to act that we have learned as an adult. We are called to an integrated life.

Linda Marks,
LIVING WITH VISION
Reclaiming the Power of the Heart

Creative people question their own and others' assumptions. They don't buy prefabricated answers to the basic questions of life. The self–renewal of creative people involves snapping out of one way of seeing and doing things and creating a new one.

Alfonso Montuori & Isabella Conti,
FROM POWER TO PARTNERSHIP:
Creating the Future of Love, Work, and Community

Creativity is . . . a major need of each human being, and the blockage of this creativity eventually threatens civilization with ultimate destruction. Humanity is therefore faced with an urgent challenge of unparalleled magnitude.

David Bohm & F. David Peat,
SCIENCE, ORDER, AND CREATIVITY:
A Dramatic New Look at the Creative Roots of Science and Life

Creation, in the arts, science, technology, and daily life, is a primary source of human realization. Creativity can replace conformity as the primary mode of social being.

Stephen Nachmanovitch,
FREE PLAY:
The Power of improvisation in Life and the Arts

*I*n beginning this chapter, I find I am rather hesitant, even a bit nervous, about writing my thoughts at this point in time. A last chapter seems so final, when of course it is no such thing. I think of Oprah Winfrey's page in her magazine "O" where she comments on the things she knows "for sure"; my problem is that what I know for sure today I may not know so surely tomorrow.

I am also aware of a bit of anxiety, or more than a bit of anxiety, about putting myself "out there". Just a day or two ago I came across words by Alfonso Montuori (CRE-ATORS ON CREATING, Frank Barron, Alfonso Montuori, Anthea Barron, Editors) suggesting that exposing our work to public scrutiny can be a "threatening proposition". Of course I am aware that some readers may be offended or bored or even worse by my writing, so I have to expect negative as well as positive responses. Problem: having experienced a super abundance of negative criticism at home during my early years – haven't many of us? – I'm likely to duck when I see it coming. However, I am reminded of Debbie Ford's words in THE SECRET OF THE SHADOW advising us that it is time to grow up and accept the fact that some people will not like us or may even hate us. I think, too, of Brian Swimme's powerful words in THE UNIVERSE IS A GREEN DRAGON, urging us to take supernovas as our models and give expression to our passion as the "primary sacrament of the universe".

In the recent past the various media were saturated, completely saturated, with stories of John Paul II: his illness, dying, funeral mass, burial, and impending choice of his successor. As one with little or no interest in the Pope as a religious leader, I have felt affronted by this inundation of information which is irrelevant to my spiritual well–being. In fact, I consider the idolizing of externals, i.e. persons, institutions and ideologies, as a sign of sickness in our society. One priest confessed, on television during these events, his great joy that his Hispanic parishioners demonstrated such faith in the Pope, such faith in the Church. He made no mention of faith in a living Spirit, but only in a fallible person and a fallible institution.

If I had an opportunity to make just one statement, it would be that our very life depends on our trusting in a living creative spirit, with a continuing openness to new experience, learning and change. No set ideology is equal to the challenges of our times, as should be abundantly apparent by the present state of the world. Religious, political, economic, environmental, cultural, educational and nationalistic ideologies have led us into all kinds of disasters including wars, famines, and incomprehensible acts of genocide. How long must we wait before we awaken to the urgency of our predicament and the desperate need for a dramatic change in perception?

Riane Eisler and David Loye have contrasted dominator societies with partnership societies, those enacting "power over" with those embracing "power with". Alfonso Montuori and Isabella Conti speak of an emerging paradigm, a major shift in perception, which "encourages us to write our own scenario and to create for ourselves our life story in a spirit of partnership with the world around us". In contrast, many religious fundamentalists believe they have not only the right but a god–commanded obligation to force their ideological perspective on everyone else. The present conflict between closed–minded ideologues and open–minded learners may be the most crucial conflict in today's world.

Actions based on rigid ideologies range from terrorist acts ("Kill the infidels!") to less lethal but nevertheless divisive and often harmful behaviors. Current issues in the United States include same–sex marriage, pro–choice rights, the medical use of marijuana, the "under God" clause in the Pledge of Allegiance, and the display of the Ten Commandments on government property. The Ten Commandments are a rigid, static definition of the will of God as interpreted by the early Hebrews, which stand in stark contrast to a dynamic awareness of an informing Spirit as suggested by Jesus.

A key issue in various religious ideologies is the variety of definitions of god. It is these definitions of god which are worshipped rather than a living Spirit, and which are the basis for beliefs and behaviors. With this issue in mind, I wrote the following four or five years ago.

Will The Real God Please Stand Up?

WHY IS IT THAT, AS we enter the third millennium, so many residents of our planet continue to accept without questioning so many different definitions of god and so many different requirements supposedly laid on human beings by those different gods? Can we really believe in such a capricious Spirit of the universe, one that lays different trips on the adherents of different religions as a price of salvation or some other holy reward? Are we unable to acknowledge the terrible price we pay in insisting that there is only one right definition of the divine and only one right path to holiness?

One of the most damaging aspects of this approach to religion is a very limited and limiting understanding of the nature of human beings, which results in all kinds of personal and social disasters. The insistence of some of the major religions on such explanations as having to work out karma or be "redeemed" by the sacrificial death of a savior, places the emphasis on the need to overcome "badness" or "sinfulness". In clinging to their old concepts, they reject current information indicating that much mental illness, addiction and criminal activity is in fact a consequence of severe psychological and spiritual damage done to children in their formative years and often continuing into adulthood. Many religions speak of the soul, but fail to acknowledge that the most important developmental task of children is to give expression to their souls in ways that fulfill their unique potential as valuable and spiritual human beings.

A recent newspaper article described a young Muslim woman studying economics in a graduate program at a large university. As is the custom with some (certainly not all) women of her religion, she covers herself except her eyes. She explained that her reason for doing this is that she is "a slave of God". By whose definition of God? A prophet who lived hundreds of years ago defined God according to his own understanding at that particular time and in light of his own needs, and his followers have been stuck with that definition – with some additions and subtractions, according to recent research – ever since.

Needless to say, Islam is not the only religion with this problem. Many religions make idols of the concepts of God introduced by their founders and often amended by their followers to suit their own needs and level of understanding. Centuries later, followers continue to cling to static images of God in the name of tradition and as a means of security in a group membership. To question the definition of God embraced by a particular religion or sect is to risk expulsion or at least suspicion by other adherents of that belief system. Some belief communities excommunicate or "shun" those who stray from the doctrinal path, and some even pronounce death sentences for those who offend doctrinal sensibilities.

The founders of various religions certainly had insights into the nature of the human condition and of the divine mystery which were profound enough to attract many followers. However, they and their early disciples were products of their own times and cultures, and as such they (to borrow from the Apostle Paul) saw through a glass darkly, sometimes very darkly. As a consequence, their definitions of their gods were limited and limiting, requiring all manner of moralities, behaviors, rituals, diets, dress codes, doctrines and dogmas, depending on the understandings of the founders and their early followers. Especially in the case of religious fundamentalists, their beliefs are cast in stone (literally in the case of the Ten Commandments!), not subject to new understandings in the light of new knowledge about the nature of human beings, planet earth and the cosmos.

For the most part, we fail to recognize how extensively our restricting concepts of the nature of the Divine permeate our society, not only in education, but in business, law, health practices, social customs, etc. We fail to acknowledge what a negative effect religious indoctrination, both overt and covert, has on other areas of life. It is as though there is some commonly accepted taboo against questioning the validity of various definitions of God as though we were questioning the existence of the Divine, when nothing could be further from the truth. In the case of agnostics and even atheists, many if not most have turned their backs on a god who never existed anyway. They have found the god of their childhood to be too small.

Eleven Commitments

Several years ago, when my husband talked me into attending an anniversary celebration at the country church of his childhood, I made use of our driving time of an hour or two to write out my current thinking concerning the nature of God (always subject to alteration of course). The church service, by the way, proved to be better than anticipated, with the speaker of the day a former pastor who delivered more of a humorous talk than a sermon. In addition, my husband had the good fortune to connect with a woman in her nineties who had been his first grade teacher.

Eleven Commitments For Becoming A Newspirit:

(not written in stone)

1.   There is a living, creating **SPIRIT** of all that is – the heart, mind, and soul of creation – and we will place your full trust in this **SPIRIT**.

2.   We will honor **SPIRIT** by being true to our own soul–selves and following the leading of **SPIRIT** in the core o f our being.

3.   We will always be open to new understanding of **SPIRIT**, never making idols of existing doctrines and dogmas, roles and rituals.

4.   We will honor our forebears by following our own unique paths, never conforming to others' ideas of what we should do and be.

5.   We will express our sexuality only in relationships of openness, honesty, equality and respect, caring for our partners as whole persons, heart and mind, body and soul.

6.   We will receive payment for our right livelihood in accordance with our needs, freely sharing our spiritual and material well–being with our neighbors.

7.   We will be open and honest in our relationships, within ourselves and with others, expressing our own thoughts and feelings and also listening with heart to the thoughts and feelings of others.

8.   We will nurture, never kill, the spirit of creative life in all beings, especially our children, setting boundaries within which they may become strong, true and loving so-cial beings.

9.   We will seek healing for ourselves and for others, that the wounds of the past may be redeemed for our present aliveness and relationships, and for our future experiences.

10. We will care deeply for planet Earth and the atmosphere which surrounds it, defending it against all harm and contributing to its health as the magnificent home which feeds and sustains us.

11. In building on our strengths, acknowledging our weaknesses, and sharing our gifts with others, we are co–creators with **SPIRIT** as we work and play in love and gratitude for the wholeness/holiness of **LIFE**.

Thoughts as of August 2005

So **what thoughts are of** greatest importance to me at this point in time? I've stated them all in the previous pages, but perhaps a summing up is useful.

- First and foremost is the ultimate need to trust the creative process of life so that we can find the freedom to be fully ourselves, encouraging others to do the same. Only then can we experience the power and oneness of creative spirit in our work, play and relationships.

- It is crucial that we let go of the external security of ideologies, committing ourselves to open–system thinking, paying attention to our intuitive awareness, and exposing our beliefs to the fresh air of experience and the ideas of others.

- In order not to "die an unlived life" (Dawna Markova's phrase), we must search out our own unique gift(s) and devote our time, energy and resources to nothing less as our contribution to our communities and our planet. We need to let go of tasks and projects which demand less of us than what we have to give.

- It is essential that we really listen to our children, hearing their fears, pains, angers and sorrows as well as their joys and excitements. We need to acknowledge their own rythms, not forcing them into patterns which cause them to deny their own reality. Only then will we be able to prevent future violence to themselves and others.

- We must remember that we are fallible human beings and that our goal is wholeness, not perfection. We will make mistakes, sometimes losing our way and wandering in a wilderness. The sooner we recognize and acknowledge our predicament, the sooner we can find our way once again.

- We need to pay close attention to the body/mind connection, again remembering that health is wholeness, not perfection. We need to ask ourselves in what ways we may be sending negative, life–denying messages to our immune system.

- Since we are dependent on a healthy Planet Earth for our own health, we must become ever more aware of ways we are damaging the earth and its ecosystems so that we can take the needed steps to change our ways. We are all responsible for caring for the earth and its inhabitants.

There is so much more I want to say (another book is "in progress") and so much more to learn. At age eighty, I can't help but wonder how much time I have left in this life. My husband and many close friends have died in recent years, so I am very much aware of illness and mortality issues. Even so, the thought – and feeling – of "not being" is beyond my comprehension. For now, I aim to be as fully alive as I am able, and that includes being open to new possibilities, perhaps even a life–enhancing partner relationship. At the same time, I remind myself of the title of Eda LeShan's book, "it's better to be over the hill than under it".

A Call to Life

In this time of personal, social, ecological, and spiritual crisis, it is of the utmost urgency that we move away from our dividing and fragmenting definitions of God. It is time to explore anew the Divine Mystery, the Great Spirit, the Creative Spirit which is beyond definition and which is available to all as the very Life of the Cosmos, including ourselves.

The Transforming Fire

Spirit is the essence of the new era being created

A NEW SPIRIT IS BURSTING forth everywhere. The Industrial Era, which has defined our reality since the Renaissance (the last major social transformation in our historical experience) is now coming to an end. This modern age with its rational, reductionist mindset, its patriarchal patterns of power and dominance, and its materialistic, competitive values has reached its limits to growth. These patterns and values brought with them great material and scientific progress; but it is this very success that is turning the Industrial Era into a nightmare. We must let it go.

Let us give it a grand funeral, and get on with the task of co–creating a future that will be joyful, loving and life–enhancing. Let us not throw out this vast accumulated knowledge, but instead liberate it from the narrow confines of the modern mindset and redefine it in the new mode of dynamic wholeness and connection.

Spirituality is at the very core of this exercise. For spirit is not only the connecting energy that will weave back together again the pieces cut asunder by the reductionist, materialist drivers of the modern era. It is the very essence of the new era we are creating.

The old Hebrew definition for spirit was "to breathe", and the Latin word *spiritus* meant breathing or wind – the breath of life. The Chinese used the word *Ch'I* to mean wind, breath, fire, and essence. Like breath, the spirit is always there even if we are not aware of it. Like wind, it can be a gentle breeze or a massive force; like fire, it can light our way and heat our bodies – or destroy everything in its path.

The way we have defined spirit or spirituality in the Modern era reflects the dominant characteristics of this age. Because spirit is not material – you can't see it, touch it, or count it – it was not considered important. Because the direct experience of spirit was denied to us, we did not trust ourselves to know good. We needed the scripture, the priest, the guru, or the scientist to tell us what to do.

There is deeply imbedded in all of us a very real and understandable fear of (the) shadow side of spirituality. Unless we embrace this and work through it, it will be very difficult for us to reclaim our spiritual gifts.

And these gifts of the spirit are many. Through the healing powers of the spirit, we can *heal* ourselves and our planet, reconnect our lives and our communities. Spirit will *empower* us, because spirit *is* inner power. And finally, spirit will *reenchant* the world with its mysterious and magical qualities. With spirit will come humility to honor that which we do not understand; a realization that there is not one right way, nor one right answer; and acceptance of the irony of all existence; and an understanding that reality is made up of opposites balancing and dancing with each other – the ongoing Cosmic Journey.

But we cannot accept these gifts without also accepting responsibility for their use. The shadow side of community can be deadening conformity. The shadow side of empowerment can be arrogance. Passion can turn into fanaticism. And mystery without understanding can be kooky or terrorizing. Even the healing power of the spirit must be tempered with knowing when *not* to heal, for to relish life is to accept death. This may be particularly true for the decaying social structures we are all caught in: it is time to let them die so there can be a new resurrection.

When Prometheus stole fire from the Gods and gave it to humans, we lost the innocence of other animals. We are different, and we have a special role to play in evolution, particularly in the profound transformation we are now going through. This is the irony of the Promethean gift to humans: we must tend the fire or it will rage out of control.

The Great Spirit is counting on us. She has given us all of the resources we need, and He is challenging us to leap. It will not be easy; but each of us has our own small part to play. And play it we will, for the Genie is out of the bottle and can't be put back in. Too many of us have gotten a glimpse of how powerful we really are. Together we are dreaming a future – a future that we now know is possible.

Suggestions For Further Reading

OVER MY DESK ARE THREE twelve–foot shelves of books of inspired writing by a great diversity of authors. I would like to include all these writings in this listing, but that would require another book and might be so overwhelming as to be useless. Following are some of the authors who have encouraged me along the way. In the case of a few books which are out of print but are too valuable to exclude from this list, you may find them in libraries or as used copies through Internet booksellers. Best wishes for great explorations.

Walter Truett Anderson, THE UPSTART SPRING, *Esalen and the American Awakening; Addison–Wesley, 1983. I have included this book because Esalen Institute, a growth center on the spectacular Big Sur Coast ot California, played an important part in my life in 1965 and 1966. This is a fascinating story of Esalen and the sixties.*

Donald Hatch Andrews, THE SYMPHONY OF LIFE; *Unity Press, 1966.While in Florida during my father's dying days, I read a report in the local paper of a fascinating talk by a professor at Florida Atlantic University. I sought out the author (retired as chemistry professor at Johns Hopkins) between classes and learned of this remarkable book to be published that same year on music and rhythm as our spiritual essence.*

Frank Barron, CREATIVITY AND PERSONAL FREEDOM; *D. Van Nostrand Co., Inc., 1968.This is one of the very interesting earlier books on the psychology of creativity, written while the author was a research psychologist at the Institute of Personality Assessment and Research, University of California, Berkeley.*

NO ROOTLESS FLOWER, An Ecology of Creativity; *Hampton Press, Inc., 1995. This is an absolutely delightful volume, written after the author's retirement as professor of psychology at the University of California, Santa Cruz Through his very personal reporting, we become familiar with both creativity and life as his passions. (Years earlier, I had wanted so much to meet him that I invited him to join me for lunch at Hotel Santa Cruz.)*

Frank Barron, Alfonso Montuori, Anthea Barron, Eds.,CREATORS ON CREATING, *Awakening and Cultivating the Imaginative Mind: Jeremy P. Tarcher/Putnam, 1997. This book offers insight and inspiration from a wide variety of unusually creative persons, with thoughtful introductions to each section.*

Claudia Bepko and Jo–Ann Krestan, SINGING AT THE TOP OF OUR LUNGS, *Women, Love, and Creativity; HarperCollins, 1993. The authors propose that passion and creativity are essential to the empowerment of women in breaking through cultural restrictions.*

Phillip L. Berman, THE COURAGE TO GROW OLD, *Forty–one prominent men and women reflect on growing old, with the wisdom and experience that comes from a rich and varied life; Ballantine/Random House, 1989. The sub-title says it all.*

Thomas Berry, THE DREAM OF THE EARTH; *Sierra Club Books, 1993. The author, a Passionist priest of exceptional and inspiring vision, has urged us to care deeply and actively for the health of our planet, both in his writings and in seminar presentations. He and physicist Brian Swimme have often co–presented their ideas and concerns.*

David Bohm and F. David Peat, SCIENCE, ORDER AND CREATIVITY, A *Dramatic New Look at the Creative Roots of Science and Life: Bantam Books, 1987. I was so drawn to the authors' ideas in this book that I arranged to meet with David Peat when he was living in Ottawa, Canada. His more recent writings continue to stimulate our thinking.*

James F. T. Bugental, Ed., THE CHALLENGES OF HUMANISTIC PSY-CHOLOGY; *McGraw–Hill Book Co., 1967. A bringing together in one vol-ume of many of the earlier "Third Force" humanistic psychologists, these writers provided great inspiration as I undertook graduate study in the fall of 1967. A gifted psychotherapist and writer, the author served as the first president of the (American) Association for Humanistic Psychology.*

Fritjof Capra, THE TAO OF PHYSICS, *An Exploration of the Parallels Between Modern Physics and Eastern Mysticism; Shambhala, 1975. This is an in–depth study of the similarities of the "cosmic dance" of an organic universe as viewed through the perspectives of modern physicists and Eastern religious mystics, a philosophical view of science.* THE TURNING POINT, *Science, Society, and* the Rising Culture; Simon & Schuster, 1982; Bantam Books, 1983. I especially appreciate Chapter 9, "The systems View of Life', which includes discussion on self–consistency the dynamics of self–transcendence, and the "co–evolution of organism plus environment".

Riane Eisler, THE POWER OF PARTNERSHIP, Seven Relationships That Will Change Your Life; New World Library, 2002. The author of THE CHALICE AND THE BLADE gives us a volume of wisdom for finding our partnership way in a violent, dominator–oriented world; a guide to personal and social transformation.

David N. Elkins, BEYOND RELIGION, A Personal Program for Building a Spiritual Life Outside the Walls of Traditional Religion; Quest Books, 1998. I first met David Elkins, a professor of educational psychology, at a conference where I appreciated having time with him and hearing of his personal journey from restrictive religious belief to life–enhancing spirituality. This book is a valuable expression of what he has learned along the way.

Marilyn Ferguson, THE AQUARIAN CONSPIRACY, Personal and Social Transformation in Our Time; J. P. Tarcher, 1980. In the Foreword to this book, John Nesbitt says that it was ahead of its time, so it is well worth reading now for information and inspiration. Be sure to read Marilyn Ferguson's Afterword.

Debbie Ford, THE SECRET OF THE SHADOW, The Power of Owning Your Whole Story; HarperSanFrancisco, 2003. The author gives us stories, insights, and tools for transforming self–defeating thoughts and feelings into possibilities for spiritual and emotional growth.

Matthew Fox, A SPIRITUALITY CALLED COMPASSION; Harper & Row, 1990. The author, a long–time Dominican priest who was excommunicated for his so–called heretical, i.e. wonderful, ideas, writes eloquently on his vision of real spirituality. I especially appreciate his chapter on "Creativity and Compassion" , an inseparable combination.

John W. Gardner, SELF–RENEWAL, The Individual and the Innovative Society; Harper & Row, 1963. The author, with various callings as college psychology professor, U. S. Secretary of Health, Education, and Welfare, and founder of Common Cause, wrote of the urgent need for creativity as way of life both for person and community. It was an exciting and fulfilling experience for me to read this book as early as 1964.

Jack R. Gibb, TRUST, a New View of Personal and Organizational Development; Guild of Tutors Press, 1978. The author cites trust as the key to personal and societal change, and refers to spirituality as the expression of trust, especially in the natural processes of life. His first chapter on the nature of trusting is essential reading

Daniel Goleman, Paul Kaufman, Michael Ray, THE CREATIVE SPIRIT (companion to the PBS television series); Dutton/Penguin, 1992.This is an absolutely delightful volume on the theme of "liberating the creative spirit within you", with practical exercises, inspiring stories from around the world, and colorful pictures and cartoons.

Tom Harpur, THE PAGAN CHRIST, Recovering the Lost Light. Thomas Allen, 2004. The author, newspaper columnist, former Anglican priest, seminary professor, shares with us his personal explorations into a "cosmic faith based on ancient truths that the modern church has renounced'. This is important thought–provoking reading of scholarly thought.

Cliff Havener, MEANING, The Secret of Being Alive; Beaver's Pond Press, 1999. The author speaks of persons as "normative' or "integrative" in their ways of thinking and being, the former committed to linear and closed system approaches, the later to dynamic, open–system waysof addressing life. He tells many interesting true stories illustrating why the creative, integrative mode is so important to a life of meaning. Most unfortunately, Cliff died soon after the publication of his book.

Jean Houston, A PASSION FOR THE POSSIBLE, A Guide to Realizing Your True Potential; HarperSanFrancisco, 1997. Jean Houston, who inspires and enlightens with both her written and spoken words, urges us to respond to the call of our own unique center, to become the most we are capable of becoming. Questions and exercises help us along the way. The author has written many more fascinating books, including A MYTHIC LIFE: Learning to Live Our Greater Story; HarperSanFranciso, 1997.

Daisaku Ikeda, Rene Simard, Guy Bourgeault. ON BEING HUMAN, Where Ethics, Medicine and Spirituality Converge; Les Presses de L'Universite de Montreal, 2002; Middleway Press, 2003. This is a most remarkable discussion between three educators/researchers on issues of great concern in our current culture.

Sidney M. Jourard, THE TRANSPARENT SELF; D. Van Nostrand, 1964, Revised Edition, 1972. This was the second book I read by a humanistic psychologist (after Carl Rogers' ON BECOMING A PERSON) and was so taken with what *the author had to say about the urgent need for personal authenticity that I began a correspondence with him, and subsequently invited him to speak to our group in Walnut Creek, California, following a week–end seminar at Esalen Institute.*

Ann Jauregui, EPIPHANIES, A *Psychotherapist's Tales of Spontaneous Emotional Healing; Prima/Crown/Random House, 2003. Integrating psychology and spirituality in the meeting of therapist and client, the author relates stories of transforming moments in the healing process Her wide–ranging thoughts and personal experiences greatly enrich the telling.*

Charles M. Johnston, THE CREATIVE IMPERATIVE, A *Four–Dimensional Theory of Human Growth &Planetary Evolution; Celestial Arts, 1986. First an artist, then a doctor and psychiatrist, the author provides much food for thought in promoting creative thinking and living as the most urgent need of our time. He is director of the Institute for Creative Development in Seattle.*

George B. Leonard, WALKING ON THE EDE OF THE WORLD, A *Memoir of the Sixties and Beyond; Houghton Mifflin, 1988. In writing which is both history and a personal journey, this one–time editor of LOOK Magazine gives us a quite enthralling moving picture of an unusual period in American cultural history.*

Anne Morrow Lindbergh, GIFT FROM THE SEA; *Pantheon Books/Random House, 1977. A very special book for meditation and inspiration, the author has given us a truly valuable gift to be revisited many times over the years. The 50ᵗʰ Anniversary Edition includes and introduction by her daughter, Reeve Lindbergh.*

Linda Marks, LIVING WITH VISION, *Reclaiming the Power of the Heart; Knowledge Systems, Inc., 1989. My extensive underlining in this book is an indication of my enthusiasm for Linda Marks' personal stories and ways of expressing and integrating issues of vision, creativity, spirituality, and passion for both individuals and organizations, As Hazel Henderson writes in the Foreword, it " can be a companion in your personal adventure".*

Dawna Markova, I WILL NOT DIE AN UNLIVED LIFE, *Reclaiming Purpose andPassion; Conari Press, 2000. This is another remarkable personal story of coming home to the self, beautifully told and including well–chosen quotes to enhance the inspirational quality of the book .In addition, the design of the book is a delight to the eye.*

Abraham Maslow, THE FARTHER REACHES OF HUMAN NATURE; Viking Press, 1971. This collection of papers was planned by the author for publication, but was published posthumously following his sudden death in 1970. Of special interest to me are the chapters on "The Creative Attitude" and "Theory Z", the latter having to do with persons he calls "transcenders". The book is a gold mine of provocative ideas.

Alfonso Montuori and Isabella Conti, FROM POWER TO PARTNERSHIP, Creating the future of Love, Work, and Community; HarperSanFrancisco, 1993. The authors explore the implications of the partnership model in many areas of life, including science, business, and the arts. They emphasize the relationship between partnership and creativity.

Oriah Mountain Dreamer, OPENING THE INVITATION, The Poem That Has Touched Lives Around the World; HarperSanFrancisco/HarperCollins, 2004. In this special little book, the author tells us a very personal story of her life, how she came to write THE INVITATION, and of many touching responses to this prose poem from persons in different life situations across the world. A most inspiring read.

Clark Moustakis, CREATIVITY AND CONFORMITY; D. Van Nostrand, 1967. This is a book which has spoken to me over the years concerning creativity as way of life. The author's words of wisdom cover such topics as ethical and moral value, self–doubt and self–inquiry. A favorite quote: "Failure to actualize essential capacities is equivalent to not being."

Stephen Nachmanovitch, FREE PLAY, The Power of Improvisation in Life and the Arts; Jeremy P. Tarcher, 1990. This is one of my favorite books of all time, both educational and inspirational. It was a gift from a dear friend, and I return to it over and over again. A quote totally relevant to our present time: "There are addictions to outmoded dogmas, for which people are massacring each other the world over."

Barbara O'Brien, OPERATORS AND THINGS, The Inner Life of a Schizophrenic: Arlington Books, 1958; Sphere Books, 1976. This author's personal story of healing helps us to understand the relationship between her creativity and her illness, her choice to be a "bronco" rather than a trained horse.

Diarmuid O'Murchu, RECLAIMING SPIRITUALITY; Crossroad Publishing, 1997 1999. RELIGION IN EXILE, A Spiritual Homecoming; Crossroad Publishing, 2000. These two volumes by a former Roman Catholic priest are essential reading for those seeking to move from from the deadness of restrictive *religion to the aliveness of spirituality. The first chapter in RELIGION IN EXILE includes the author's personal story.*

Parker J. Palmer, THE ACTIVE LIFE, *Wisdom for Work, Creativity, and Caring; HarperSanFrancisco. This book was my introduction to Parker Palmer's life and thinking, in which he tells of trying the monastic life and finding that it was not for him. Many will be able to identify with him, as I did.* LET YOUR LIFE SPEAK, *Listening for the Voice of Vocation; Jossey–Bass/Wiley, 2000. I seem to identify more closely with the personal story and thoughts of the author in this book than in any other, likely because there are so many parallels with my own life. His personal story, including his emerging from depression, is especially inspiring. A* HIDDEN WHOLE-NESS, *The Journey Toward an Undivided Life; Jossey–Bass/Wiley, 2004. This book is a further expansion on the Importance of being our real, undivided selves and of community, such as a "circle of trust", where we can express our wholeness. Note: Another Palmer book,* THE COURAGE TO TEACH, *Exploring the Inner Landscape of a Teacher's Life (Jossey–Bass, 1998), will be of special interest to educators, formal and otherwise.*

Anna Quindlen, A SHORT GUIDE TO A HAPPY LIFE; *Random House, 2000. This is indeed a very short book, but one of encou aging, life–enhancing thoughts and exceptionally heart–touching photos.*

Rachel Naomi Remen, KITCHEN TABLE WISDOM, *Stories That Heal; Riverhead Books, 1997;* MY GRANDFATHER'S BLESSINGS, *Stories of Strength, Refuge, and Belonging, Riverhead Books, 2000. Here are two very special volumes of life–changing stories that touch heart, mind, and soul by a physician–healer.*

Lois Robbins, WAKING UP! IN THE AGE OF CREATIVITY; *Bear & Co., 1985. My husband and I discovered this unique volume in Calgary, Alberta, and proceeded to read it to each other while on the road to California. I was so enthusiastic about the discussion of some of Matthew Fox's ideas and the value of "extrovert meditation" that I contacted the author/artist, who then became a dear friend.*

Carl Rogers, ON BECOMING A PERSON; *Houghton Mifflin, 1961. The principal of my son's elementary school introduced me to this, my first book on the subject of humanistic psychology. Finally, a personal story and a psychology with which I could identify! I especially appreciate the first chapter, "This Is Me", in which the author says "I could not work in a field (religion) where I would be required to believe in some specified religious doctrine." He left the seminary to study psychology.*

Natalie Rogers, THE CREATIVE CONNECTION, *Expressive Arts as Healing; Science & Behavior Books, 1993. In this beautiful book, Natalie has brought together in herself and in her writing the "person–centered approach" of her father Carl and the artistic talent of her mother Helen. This is an exceptional volume of stories, illustrations, and applications of expressive arts for healing.*

Theodore Roszak, WHERE THE WASTELAND ENDS, *Politics and Transcendence in Postindustrial Society; Anchor/Doubleday, 1973. The author writes about perhaps the most critical issue of our times, "the religious dimension of political life', and by religious he means what many call spiritual, "vision born of transcendent knowledge".* UNFINISHED ANIMAL, *The Aquarian Frontier and the Evolution of Consciousness; Harper & Row, 1975. This is an excellent consideration of the possibility of a major shift in human consciousness, although some of the symptoms of such an evolutionary shift may seem unlikely clues.* PERSON/PLANET, *The Creative Disintegration of Industrial Society; Anchor/Doubleday, 1979. This is another excellent exploration into human consciousness, this time with a focus on personal authenticity and human potential as affecting our commercial and political culture.* THE VOICE OF THE EARTH; *Simon & Schuster, 1993. This is an extensive and urgent consideration of the interrelationship between the health of the planet and the human psyche, a passionate plea for our attention to the ecological/ psychological crisis.*

John Shelby Spong, WHY CHRISTIANITY MUST CHANGE OR DIE, *A Bishop Speaks to Believers in Exile; HarperSanFrancisco, 1999. A retired Episcopal bishop offers an excellent analysis of what ails the Christian religion and what is needed if it is to recover.*

Gloria Steinem, REVOLUTION FROM WITHIN, *A book of Self–Esteem; Little, Brown & Co., 1991. This book is a most important read for those wondering about the difference between what Gloria Steinem calls situational self–esteem and core self–esteem, what I have referred to as performance self–esteem and soul self–esteem. The spiritual implications are tremendous for our personal and political lives.*

Brian Swimme, THE UNIVERSE IS A GREEN DRAGON. *A Cosmic Creation Story; Bear & Co., 1985. This is a book to which I return time and again for inspiration. In the form of questioning dialogue, the author calls us to* "*adventurous play*", with the way of the universe as our model and celebration as our response to the beauty of the cosmos.

Pierre Teilhard de Chardin, THE PHENOMEN OF MAN; Wm. Collins, 1959; Harper & Row, 1965. When I read this book in the late 1960s, my lack of relevant scientific background made it tough going, but it was well worth the effort in opening my mind to the idea of our continuing evolution. Teilhard's vision is exciting. A Roman Catholic priest, he was forbidden to publish his ideas during his lifetime.

WITH THANKS

To the following for their permission to quote from copyrighted works:

James F. T. Bugental, CHALLENGES OF HUMANISTIC PSYCHOLOGY; McGraw–Hill Book Co., 1967

David Bohm and F. David Peat, SCIENCE, ORDER, AND CREATIVITY, A Dramatic New Look at the Creative Roots of Science and Life, Bantam Books, 1987

Fritjof Capra, THE TURNING POINT, Science, Society, and the Rising Culture; Simon and Schuster, 1982, Bantam Books, 1983

Cliff Havener, MEANING, The Secret of Being Alive; Beaver's Pond Press, Inc., 1999

Linda Marks, LIVING WITH VISION, Reclaiming the Power of the Heart; Knowledge Systems, Inc., 1989

Alfonso Montuori and Isabella Conti, FROM POWER TO PARTNERSHIP, Creating the Future of Love, Work, and Community; HarperSanFrancisco, 1993

Stephen Nachmanovitch, FREE PLAY, The Power of Improvisation in Life and The Arts; Jeremy P. Tarcher, Inc., 1990

Charles M. Johnston, THE CREATIVE IMPERATIVE, A Four–Dimensional Theory of Human Growth and Planetary Evolution; Celestial Arts, 1986

Diarmuid O'Murchu, RECLAIMING SPIRITUALITY, A New Spiritual Framework For Today's World; The Crossroad Publishing Co., 1999 RELIGION IN EXILE, A Spiritual Homecoming; The Crossroad Publishing Co., 2000

Parker J. Palmer, THE ACTIVE LIFE, Wisdom for Work, Creativity, and Caring; HarperSanFrancisco, 1991

THE COURAGE TO TEACH, Exploring the Inner Landscape of a Teacher's Life; Jossey–Bass, Inc., 1998

LET YOUR LIFE SPEAK, Listening for the Voice of Vocation; Jossey–Bass/John Wiley & Sons, Inc., 2000

A HIDDEN WHOLENESS, The Journey toward an Undivided Life; Jossey–Bass/John Wiley & Sons, Inc., 2004

Theodore Roszak, WHERE THE WASTELAND ENDS, Politics and Transcen–dence in Postindustrial Society; Anchor Books/Doubleday & Co., 1973, PERSON/PLANET, The Creative Disintegration of Industrial Society; Anchor Press/Doubleday, 1978/1979

Note: *The following authors are deceased, their books are out of print, their publishers did not respond to my requests, and I could not locate copyright holders. However, I knew both authors personally and know that they would want their words included.*

Donald Hatch Andrews, THE SYMPHONY OF LIFE; Unity Books, 1966

Jack R. Gibb, TRUST, a New View of Personal and Organizational Development; Guild of Tutors Press, 1978.

WITH THANKS

To the following who have contributed so much to the preparation of this book:

Linda Mary Gregson, former student, long–time friend and colleague, and co–editor of many books, for editorial assistance and proof–reading;

Noelle Tangredi, graphic artist and computer wizard (well, compared to me anyway), for art work and computer expertise;

Coleen Clay Clark, friend of many years, musician, photographer, for her photograph of the author;

Paul Liebau, long–time friend and occasional housemate, teacher, counselor, writer, publisher, for reading and critiquing the manuscript;

The staff of Trafford Publishing for 'mid–wifing' this book to publication;;

George Leonard and Troy Chapman for encouragement to quote from their non–copyrighted words. (*Note: Information about Troy is available at* friendsoftroy.org, *or you can write to him:* Troy Chapman, 169076, Kinross Correctional Facility, 16770 Watertower Dr., Kincheloe, MI 49788, U.S.A.

Deborah Levine Herman with Cynthia Black, for their especially helpful book, SPIRITUAL WRITING, from Inspiration to Publication; Beyond Words Publishing, 2002.

The many authors (and several wives of authors) who, along with granting permission to quote, have sent words of encouragement;

And to all those who have provided caring along the way:

Shirley Neville and the staff, volunteers, and program participants at Third Age Outreach (St. Joseph's Health Care London) for their enthusiasm over many years;

Outstanding teachers, most of whom are now deceased, including Sunday school teacher Mrs. Loomis; elementary school teacher Mrs. Hubbard (reader of exciting poetry), Laurel School teachers Florence Stowell and Maude Tomlin, Smith college professors Fritz Heider, William Christian, Ralph Harlow, Elsa Siipola, and Mary Ellen Chase, University of Toronto graduate school professors Allen Tough and Jo Flaherty, and fellow students all along the way;

Students and colleagues in Human Services at Fanshawe College during the 1970s; the staff of Project Worth and Senior Network Services in California; the staff and members of the Association for Humanistic Psychology during the 1980s, and the counseling staff at the London Interfaith Counselling Centre during the 1990s, many of whom have continued to be friends;

My very dear and special family, step–family, and extended family of friends in the United States, Canada and Europe, who are so important to me at this time in my life. In addition to my immediate families, friends who have urged me on include Gloria, Louise, Cay, Peggy, Cathy, Beverley, Kathy, Pat, Sheila, Nancy, Mary, Susan, Margaret, Lois, Dean, Joyce and Edna and Judith.

Printed in the United States
By Bookmasters